Praise for *The Happy Home Loan Handbook*

Buying property is hard, but Aaron Christie-David makes it so much easier. His approach to property and borrowing is practical, tried and tested – and importantly, it works.

Ben Nash, Founder of Pivot Wealth and author of *Replace Your Salary by Investing*

Aaron beautifully articulates the home loan process and fills a gap in the market, with so many books focused on the analysis of property itself. As one of Australia's leading property investors, I know that property is a game of finance. Whether you are buying a family home or an investment property, this book will guide you through the ins and outs of the process to ensure long-term success!

Steve Palise, owner of Palise Property and author of the award-winning *Commercial Property Investing Explained Simply* and *Residential Property Investing Explained Simply*

The Happy Home Loan Handbook is exactly what both property investors and owner-occupiers need right now. This handbook demystifies the process and provides you with a clear understanding of how to effectively save for a deposit and which structures to use to maximise your borrowing capacity over the long term. Most importantly, this book clearly outlines how to pay off your loan as soon as possible and get on with the job of enjoying your life. It's a must-read for anyone who has a home loan or is looking to buy a property and have a home loan in the future.

Paul Glossop, Managing Director of Pure Property Investment and author of *A Surfer's Guide to Property Investing*

In *The Happy Home Loan Handbook*, Aaron Christie-David masterfully demystifies the often-intimidating process of securing a home loan. This book is not just about securing a loan – it's about laying the foundations for a happy, fulfilling life in your new home. Aaron's book stands out as an essential guide, offering a wealth of practical advice wrapped in an engaging narrative.

Michael Yardney, Founder of Metropole Property Group

I read this book from cover to cover in one sitting. As a real estate agent, business owner, homeowner and investor from an early age, I found this book well articulated and educational, especially for those starting their journey of buying their own h~~~

Trever Molenaar, Director of m

This book is dedicated to my supportive and beautiful wife Bernadette and my two wonderful daughters, Sienna and Zara. Thank you for believing in me.

THE HAPPY HOME LOAN HANDBOOK

GET YOUR LOAN APPROVED, BUY YOUR DREAM HOME AND ENJOY YOUR LIFE

AARON CHRISTIE-DAVID

MAJOR
STREET

Published in 2024 by Major Street Publishing Pty Ltd
info@majorstreet.com.au | +61 406 151 280 | majorstreet.com.au

© Aaron Christie-David 2024
The moral rights of the author have been asserted.

A catalogue record for this book is available
from the National Library of Australia

Printed book ISBN: 978-1-922611-97-0
Ebook ISBN: 978-1-922611-98-7

Cover design by Typography Studio
Internal design by Production Works
Printed in Australia by Griffin Press

10 9 8 7 6 5 4 3 2 1

Disclaimer

Contents

Preface

A home loan is a privilege

I love Australia. Getting to call this country home is one of the biggest blessings in my life, and buying a piece of it is an achievement I'm proud of. My background is Sri Lankan, and I've been back to Sri Lanka on a few occasions. It's a nation with great history, rich culture and amazing hospitality and people, but it has been plagued by civil war, economic turmoil and crippling levels of debt. Australia is lucky enough not to have these problems, which is part of why many people from around the world want to call it home.

I hope you share that desire to own your piece of this country. Our government provides support to help first home buyers get their foot in the door and start their property journey. Is it expensive to buy property in Australia? Absolutely! Is it unattainable or unaffordable? No. This topic is debated at a political level by both federal and state governments, as well as on the national news, around dinner tables and on social media. However, while some people choose to spend their time complaining about the price of real estate, a select cohort of Australians is determined to get their loan approved, buy their dream home and enjoy their life. If you are among them, then this book is for you.

There is no shortage of resources to help home buyers. There are online courses, podcasts, seminars, YouTube videos, Facebook groups, websites and books like this. With all this content out there, why do so many potential home buyers lack confidence in their ability to buy a property? I don't feel that it's a lack of resources; rather, it's a lack of resourcefulness.

As much as you can learn from others, you learn more from making mistakes, and I've made my fair share! I bought my first unit opposite a cemetery. I bought my second unit in a high-density development overlooking a busy train station. I bought my third property off the plan. I've since sold all these properties (and none at a loss), and my wife and I own our family home in Woonona, about 20 minutes north of Wollongong. We have also purchased our own commercial property for our business. I feel like all the roads I have taken have led me to this point. I failed forwards, but most importantly, I took action. The property market rewarded me for being proactive to buy, as I sold all the aforementioned properties for a profit and learned priceless lessons.

My hope for you is that you take the information you need from this book to build your confidence and knowledge of what's involved in getting your loan approved, buying your dream home and, most importantly, getting on with enjoying your life. Too often, potential home buyers are crippled with analysis paralysis and feel overwhelmed. I want to acknowledge that it's not easy, but it's not impossible, and the property market rewards action-takers and decision-makers.

Why is this book called *The Happy Home Loan Handbook*?

In 2019, I went on a family holiday to Japan, and as you do at the airport, I browsed through the latest books to pick up some light reading for the flight. My brother-in-law Damien is an avid book reader and found a book called *Happy Money* by Ken Honda. It was the best of both worlds: a money book (a genre I enjoy reading) and a Japanese author!

I love the concept of happy money. In a nutshell, Ken Honda's philosophy is that 'happy money' is money received or spent with joy, gratitude and positive intention. 'Unhappy money', on the other hand, is associated with negative emotions such as fear, greed or resentment. Ken Honda suggests that the nature of our relationship with money, whether it is happy or unhappy, significantly impacts our life experience and overall wellbeing.

I resonate so much with this ideology as a mortgage broker. Debt has a negative connotation for many people, especially home loan debt. Many people somehow believe that there's good debt (investment loans) and bad debt (home loans), and I can understand that at a professional level but I could never accept it at a deeply personal level. Why wouldn't you consider a home loan good debt? It may mean you're not renting anymore. It may mean you now have a place to call your own, being able to put down roots and own a property in this great land of ours, and never worry about having to move your family. What about the special memories that you could create in your own home – the Easter lunches, Christmas Day feasts, birthday parties and building connections with neighbours, to name a few? It could also provide the leverage and equity for you to buy investment properties and build intergenerational wealth. There is (generally) no home without a loan, especially when you're buying your first home. So, why the resistance to debt? How have we been conditioned to feel that it is better to rent because a mortgage is a life sentence where the bank somehow owns your home because they lent you the money to buy it?

My mission is to reframe the way Australian families perceive their mortgage as a 'happy home loan'. This book tells you, from start to finish, how to get your home loan approved, buy your dream home and get on with enjoying life. It takes you through the most commonly asked questions and will get you thinking about what action you need to take to make your home ownership aspirations come true.

My story

If I were to tell you I met my wife while we were both shopping at Kmart in Nowra on Boxing Day, you might think it sounds like a plot line from a Hollywood rom-com! That's exactly what happened. My best mate from school saw Bernadette, who was shopping, and called me over to tell me my future wife was standing in front of him. Little did he know this would be true!

That day changed my life forever. A Christmas holiday on the beautiful South Coast of New South Wales led to me meeting the woman of my dreams. I had recently been made redundant working in marketing for a financial services company at the height of the global financial crisis and, being unemployed, I didn't think my prospects were that red hot. The phrase 'carpe diem' (Latin for 'seize the day') came to mind, and I mustered up the courage to introduce myself and politely asked if she would like to grab a coffee.

We're now celebrating ten years of marriage, during which we have welcomed two gorgeous girls (Sienna and Zara) into the world, made a sea change from Sydney, and built and grown our business and property portfolio – and it feels like we're just getting started. It's that line from Steve Jobs that sinks in when I reflect on our life together: that you can only connect the dots by looking backward. In life, we all get sliding doors moments that set us on a different trajectory, and I'm blessed when I think about the life I've been gifted by going through this door.

Speaking of sliding doors moments, another significant moment for Bernadette and I happened when we were on holiday in Thailand and having an incredible seafood dinner. The restaurant had the most amazing reviews and was packed, and to our surprise it was run by a Sikh gentleman. He was the friendliest and most hospitable guy, and he somehow took a liking to us, and kept serving us ice cold beers all night and insisted we stay till after the restaurant closed to have a chat. I asked him how an Indian guy runs such a successful seafood restaurant in Thailand. His answer shouldn't have surprised me: work hard, serve your customers with love and enjoy what you do. He also highly recommended that we read a book called *The Richest Man in Babylon* by George Samuel Clason. We did, and that book – and the realisation it inspired in us that good money habits are timeless – sparked a series of events for us, especially when Bernie and I started to plan what we wanted out of life together and the type of lifestyle we wanted to build. It was with such clarity that Bernie said, 'Why don't you become a mortgage broker?' At this point in my life, I was working for the Commonwealth Bank of Australia in home loan distribution and marketing, specifically working with the mortgage broking channel. Previously I worked at Wizard Home Loans, so I knew about home loans, building wealth through property and the mortgage broking industry. This lit a fuse in me, and when we returned I quit my corporate role and took up mortgage broking, and I haven't looked back.

Our decision to move out of Sydney was quite easy as we knew we wanted to get off the hamster wheel of 'work, pay mortgage, sleep, repeat' and breathe. In 2018 we moved down to Thirroul, a great place on the South Coast where we rented and fell in love with the slower pace of life. Over the next few years, we were blessed with Sienna and Zara, and it was at this point that I realised, having two healthy children, a home that we had bought and the lifestyle this country offers, it doesn't get better than this. I wanted so many more Australians to enjoy the feeling of security that comes from the ability to buy your own home. It inspired me to write this book and share my journey of home ownership with the next generation of home buyers who have the aspiration but need some guidance. I know first-hand how hard it was for me and my wife to get into the property market, so I can imagine what it will be like for our two daughters when they want to buy their first home. If we're not setting the right example for them, what hope do they have?

Our goal has never been to amass a property portfolio to brag about. It's been about quality over quantity, and ensuring we are buying the right property to help us build a portfolio we can comfortably retire on and, most importantly, be able to build intergenerational wealth that our children and their children will become the beneficiaries of.

If we can do it, then we have the belief that you can do it too.

Happy reading,

Aaron Christie-David

PART I
GETTING YOUR LOAN APPROVED

Chapter 1

How to mentally prepare yourself to buy your dream home

The first step to getting your loan approved is finding the courage to embark upon the home-buying journey in the first place. This chapter covers some of the barriers that prevent people from taking the plunge and looks at ways to help you overcome them.

Is now a good time to buy?

Possibly the most common question I hear from home buyers is, 'Is now a good time to buy?' It's like asking a hairdresser if you need a haircut! It's fair to say that my world is loans and property, so naturally I have a bias towards buying a home.

The media is constantly running stories about how hard it is to buy, housing prices being out of reach for Australians and the property market being too expensive, as well as opinion pieces from property experts and the banks' economists giving mixed outlooks on the property market. All this leads to confusion, overwhelm and a lack of confidence. I'm hoping that this book will give you confidence that home ownership is attainable and achievable.

It's easy to get caught up in the sentiment that the Australian housing market is unaffordable and the Great Australian Dream is out of reach. Absolutely, it has gotten harder to get into the property market, but it's not impossible. That's the glimmer of hope I'm hoping you'll latch onto and channel to become determined to do everything within your power to get into the property market. Your future self will thank you for this decision.

Media reports on the Australian property market usually highlight the capital cities and compare indicators such as the capital growth rate year on year or the auction clearance rates, but these only tell a very small part of the story. They aren't the indicators you need to be focused on. Your goal should be to zoom right in on the area where you want to buy and learn everything you can about it. What infrastructure is being built in this community? What percentage of people own their home as opposed to renting? Which sections or streets are the most desirable? Then, zoom even closer into the properties that you can afford in this area and compare them. Which properties tend to attract more people to the inspections? Which properties sell faster than others? Which agent or agency is selling the most properties? Remember, you're not buying the whole market; you're buying a particular home, in a particular street, in a particular suburb. Narrow your focus in order to help you ignore the market commentary and buy what you can afford when you can afford to.

Buying your home is a privilege, not a right, and waiting for the government to step in and help you or for the property market to roll out the red carpet for you and say 'this is the best time to buy' is a waste of time because it just isn't going to happen. If you want to buy your home, then you need to rewire how you see the property market. If you keep telling yourself that property is unaffordable, then you're buying into this mentality. If all your friends are constantly being negative about the prospect of buying their own home, then you can either let this hold you back or choose to shut out the noise and create your own destiny.

There's a fable I love about the eagle and the chicken. The baby eagle fell from his nest and was found by a farmer, who brought the eaglet to the farm and raised him with the chickens. Growing up the eagle acted like a chicken, strutting around and pecking at the ground. A wildlife expert came to see this majestic eagle who believed he was a chicken and tried to get the eagle to fly, but he wouldn't; instead, the eagle jumped down and joined the chickens in the coop. However, the wildlife expert returned, determined to unleash the potential of the magnificent creature. He took the eagle far away to the foot of a high mountain. Here, the eagle could not see the farm or the chicken coop. The expert held the eagle on his arm and pointed high into the sky, where the sun was shining brightly, and said, 'Eagle, thou art an eagle! Stretch forth thy wings and fly'. This time the eagle's gaze went skyward into the bright sun, and he straightened his large body and stretched out his massive wings. His wings moved, slowly at first, then surely and powerfully. With the mighty screech of an eagle, he flew.

I love this story as it provides a powerful insight into the impact of your environment and the power of belief. Sometimes you need an expert to come along and believe in you. That's my hope for this book – to inspire you to shift the way you see yourself, and to light a fuse in you that home ownership is attainable with the right environment and people to support and guide you.

Changing your mindset is not an overnight process. If you can slowly rewire your brain, then it will kick your reticular activating system (RAS) into gear. The RAS is known as the gatekeeper of information between the conscious and unconscious mind. If you've had your eye on a new car, let's say a Volkswagen Golf, it's uncanny how all you notice on the road is all the Volkswagen Golfs. You start to notice all the advertisements for Volkswagen Golfs, and suddenly you're having conversations with people who bought a Volkswagen Golf and watching Volkswagen Golf reviews on YouTube. If you can activate your RAS around the belief that home ownership is attainable, that can be the conduit for you to read books like this, listen to home-buying podcasts, speak to people who have bought their home and watch informative videos on YouTube.

There are plenty of mantras you may hear when it comes it buying property, and they have some home truths to them. Let's look at a few of them:

- 'The best time to buy a home is always five years ago' – Ray Brown. This may be true but it isn't an overly positive perspective. Five years ago you may not have even been in a position to buy a property! A great way to reframe this is to buy what you can afford when you can afford to.
- 'Time in the market beats market timing every time' – Warren Buffett. I definitely concur with this sentiment. There is no perfect time to buy; it's better to get in and try to play the long game.
- 'Don't wait to buy real estate, buy real estate and wait' – Will Rogers. Like the previous saying, this refers to the fact that property is a long game and there will never be a 'perfect' time to buy.
- 'Buy land, they're not making it anymore' – Mark Twain. This has a certain truth to it, and COVID-19 did show us that having more space is valuable. However, apartment prices didn't exactly fall through the floor. It is perhaps better to focus on buying a quality property that you can afford.
- 'Buying real estate is not only the best way, the quickest way, the safest way, but the only way to become wealthy' – Marshall Field. According to the 2023 edition of the 'Rich List' published by *The Australian Financial Review*, one third of Australia's 250 richest people amassed their fortune from construction, development and property asset management. Property is

an asset class that has a strong track record, and banks are willing to lend against it.

· 'If you don't like where you are, move. You are not a tree' – Jim Rohn. I like this quote because it encapsulates such a simple truth. You always have the ability to sell your property and buy somewhere else.

Hopefully, a few of these mantras resonate with you and can help you build confidence in your home-buying journey.

The power of goal setting and visualisation

We're all aware of the poor success rate of New Year's resolutions. There is a range of statistics that does the rounds every year about how a quarter of people will abandon their New Year's resolutions after just one week. Some hope within them inspired them to change an aspect of their life, whether in relation to their finances, their health or fitness, travel or achieving a life milestone such as buying their own home. Hope got them started, but hope will only take you so far if it is not supported by planning, accountability and action.

A great research study into the power of goal setting was conducted by Dr Gail Matthews, a psychology professor at Dominican University in California. It involved 267 participants who were divided into five groups:

· The first group had to think about their goals and rate them according to various factors, but not write them down. This group achieved a 43 per cent overall success rate or progressed at least part of the way to attaining their goals.
· The second group did the same, but this group wrote down the goals.
· The third group did the same as the second but also wrote down their action commitments.

- The fourth group did all of that and also shared their action commitments with a friend.
- The final group did everything the others did but also sent their friends updates. This group had the highest success rate at 76 per cent.

A goal without a plan is simply a dream. This study highlights the importance of accountability. So many potential home buyers are afraid to share their aspirations with friends and family, as they may be told that this is a terrible time to be buying. Other doubters may ask how they're going to afford it or tell them that the property market is overpriced. Please don't be deterred by the negativity; instead, find someone who will be in your corner and support your ambitions.

Another incredibly powerful tool you can use is a 'vision board' (or, as some people like to call it, an 'action board'). If this sounds a bit woo-woo for you, stay with me – I had the same reaction when I was first introduced to this concept. The idea with a vision board is to gather images of the achievements you would like to complete; for example, if you wanted to visit Italy next year, your vision board might have images of the Amalfi Coast, wood-fired margherita pizza, gelato and the Trevi Fountain. You could keep your vision board next to the mirror you use to get ready, on the sun visor of your car or on your desk at work, or make it your desktop image on your computer or the home screen on your phone. By seeing it day in and day out, your subconscious receives signals that you're working towards an amazing trip to Italy. It won't book your plane ticket or plan out your itinerary, but it might prompt you to start doing research online, follow a few travel vloggers on YouTube and Instagram and speak to friends who have travelled to Italy. The trip now starts to feel real, and once you announce to your friends and family that you're going to Italy, your chances of going increase.

Can you imagine if you applied the same focus and discipline to buying your own home?

Parkinson's law and the importance of timeframes

'Parkinson's law' is the phenomenon that a task expands to fill the time allotted for its completion. The term was first coined by Cyril Northcote Parkinson in a 1955 article in which he details the story of a woman whose only task that day is to send a postcard – a task that would take a busy person around three minutes. However, the woman spends an hour finding the card, another half an hour searching for her glasses, 90 minutes writing the card, then 20 minutes deciding whether or not to take an umbrella along on her walk to the mailbox… and this continues until her day is filled. There's a saying that if you want a job done, give it to a busy person!

I'm sharing this story with you to encourage you think more deeply about the timeframe you're giving yourself to buy your home. Maybe it's six months, or maybe it's six years? Parkinson's law could mean that you're delaying what could be done earlier. A great litmus test for you around this is to speak with a mortgage broker or buyer's agent and find out whether you're financially able to enter the market and what you could afford to purchase. They may be able to give you some professional guidance around suitable timeframes to save for a deposit and buy a quality property, which then gives you something to work towards.

How to make your home-buying fears disappear

Buying a home is scary and intimidating. Take some reassurance that millions of Australians have done it before you and millions of Australians will do it after you, so you're not alone! Still, this doesn't change the fact that when you're going through the process of getting your loan and buying your home, there are a range of emotions that will surface, and I would say that one of the most common is fear.

There's a great TED Talk by Tim Ferriss called 'Why you should define your fears instead of your goals' that I have found particularly helpful for addressing fear. Ferriss suggests that you list out all your fears and what could go wrong. Then, list out what options you have to prevent these fears from becoming reality. Then, list out what you could do if these fears became reality. The most invaluable insight, however, is his suggestion to list out the cost of inaction over a six-month, one-year and three-year period. I highly recommend you check out this TED Talk and then put pen to paper on the fears that surface for you when you consider buying a home.

To help you get started, I've made a list of the fears that I've encountered when helping Australians buy a home:

- **Job security or income.** This may play on your mind if you're planning to get a loan and are worried about being able to make your repayments, or if you have doubts about your role long term. A good way to address this is to ensure that you have a buffer of savings – say one to three months' worth of living expenses – that you can rely on if you lose your job until you find your next opportunity.
- **Interest rates increasing.** The Reserve Bank of Australia (RBA) and your lender can raise or lower interest rates for everyone who has a loan. Yes, an interest-rate rise means your monthly repayments will increase, so if there are talks about interest rates rising then it is best to be prepared by having your savings buffer in place. This will give you the sleep-at-night factor of being sure that you can manage your mortgage repayments. In the event that interest rates go down, consider keeping your repayments at a higher level so you can pay down your loan more quickly.
- **The home's value falling.** Do you feel like you may be buying at the peak of the market and the value of your home might suddenly fall? The media have coined a term for this: 'fear of overpaying' (FOOP). Your home's value falling is something to worry about only if you are planning to sell. Learn to tune out the noise once you have bought – turn off all property

notifications and enjoy life in your new home. Alternatively, focus on finding ways to add value to your home, such as through renovations or landscaping.

· **Unexpected maintenance costs.** What if the hot water requires replacing or you start having issues with the roofing, and you're faced with an expensive repair job? If you've bought your home, welcome to weekend trips to the hardware store, DIY projects and getting to know local tradespeople! This is why it is important to have funds set aside in the event of an emergency. When faced with unexpected maintenance costs, just remember the times when you were renting and wanted to hang a piece of art or get a repair done, and the long-winded approval process you had to go through with the property manager and the landlord.

· **Strata expenses, such as special levies.** If you have purchased an apartment or a duplex with a body corporate, there may be unforeseen expenses, such as driveways needing work or plumbing issues in the common property. Special levies could arise off the back of legislative changes, such as cladding upgrades to become compliant, and this is out of your control. Again, having an emergency fund will help dampen the financial blow. No matter how much due diligence you complete on the state of the body corporate and the building before you buy, unforeseen expenses are a risk when you buy into a strata-titled property.

· **Suffering from a health issue that means you can't work for a period.** Depending on the nature of your illness, you may be covered by your personal income protection insurance. It's absolutely critical that you update your personal insurance coverage for this new debt you are taking on. You may be covered through your superannuation and think your chances of falling sick are slim, but this is a decision you'll need to consciously make and be comfortable with. The only other thing I'll say here is that health is wealth, so do what you can to look after it.

- **Fear of making a mistake (FOMM) with your purchase.** Buyer's remorse is extremely common. In fact, a study carried out by Pureprofile indicated that 45 per cent of home buyers experienced some post-purchase remorse and 21 per cent lamented lifestyle changes or having to cut back on spending to afford repayments. Other regrets buyers reported included the location of their home not being as convenient or nice as they had expected (14 per cent) and their home needing more repairs or renovations than they first anticipated (16 per cent). If you can make peace with the reality that the home you are buying isn't necessarily 'perfect', this can help to reduce your remorse and increase your happiness.

- **Fear of missing out (FOMO).** This phenomenon was prevalent during the pandemic buying craze, when properties were being purchased without even being seen or inspected. This type of behaviour is usually driven when the property market is red hot and the front-running story in the national evening news. It's hard not to get caught up in the pressure to buy when it feels like everyone else is buying, though you're going to be battling hordes of buyers and facing intense competition, especially when it comes to price.

I hope this list helps you to identify your fears and address each of them. If you are purchasing as a couple, it's important to work through each of your own fears separately and then come together to discuss your lists. Respect the other person's perspective, as they have had a different experience growing up to you, which may affect their feelings around home ownership.

Other options to consider

If you still feel like maybe you aren't ready to buy your dream home and are procrastinating or overanalysing your decisions, maybe it's time to look at alternative options and the implications these may have on your life.

Option 1: continue to rent

If you are currently renting, the path of least resistance is to continue renting. However, consider that at any point your landlord could increase the rent. This is out of your control, and you would either have to cough up the extra money or find a new place to rent. This means searching for, inspecting and applying for your next rental. It may mean moving out of the area where you would like to live and incurring the costs that come with moving places.

Think long term as well: as you continue to rent, on average Australian house prices compound by 6 per cent annually. Let's do the maths on this for a $750,000 property (see table 1.1).

Table 1.1: the value of a $750,000 property compounding at 6 per cent annually over five years

Purchase price	$750,000
Year 1	$795,000
Year 2	$842,700
Year 3	$893,262
Year 4	$946,858
Year 5	$1,003,670

Yes, you're reading that right: in five years' time, this property will be worth over $1 million. (Note that not every property across

Australia will have linear capital growth of 6 per cent annually. Some will grow more slowly – but others will grow more quickly.) There is just no way you can save for a deposit while you continue to rent and property prices continue to increase. This reality has deflated the dreams of so many prospective home buyers who continue to get priced out of the market. Also, the real icing on the cake is that rising interest rates reduce your borrowing capacity.

The longer you wait to enter the property market, the harder it becomes. I've seen time and time again families who are renting and have their children settled into schools, and then their landlord chooses to sell the property, and now they have to move and struggle to find another rental property in the area or nearby. It's never an ideal scenario. Renting will serve you for a time in your life, but it's not fun when you have to keep moving and never have the ability to put down roots long term.

Option 2: become a 'rentvestor'

'Rentvesting' is the term used to describe a strategy where you buy where you can afford to invest and rent where you want to live. The primary reason for doing this is because you cannot afford to buy into the area where you want to live.

I could write a whole book on rentvesting and the pros and cons of this strategy. Bernadette and I were rentvestors for quite some time, until our landlord gave us notice to move out when Bernadette was pregnant. There's never an ideal time, but this was terrible timing. When it was just the two of us, we had the ability to move to apartments in different areas, but now the time was right for us to buy our own place and put down roots where we wanted to raise a family. We brought forward our home ownership ambitions and made a pact that never again would we be under the power of a landlord.

Rentvesting can serve you for a time in your life, typically when you are younger and have a limited deposit and borrowing capacity.

Those who have succeeded with rentvesting have usually engaged a buyer's agent and an investment-savvy mortgage broker. This strategy can work well if you purchase in a strong growth area and your investment property greatly increases in value. The available equity then provides you with the deposit to buy your next investment property, enabling you to scale up your property portfolio.

The questions you will need to answer at some point during your rentvesting journey include the following:

- When do you plan on purchasing your primary place of residence?
- How much do you want to buy your home for?
- Where will the deposit come from to buy your home?
- Will you need to sell your investment properties, or can you draw the equity out of your investment properties?
- Does your borrowing capacity allow you to retain your investment property (or properties) and purchase your home?
- What does your cash flow position look like with all your loans and investment property expenses? Is it sustainable?
- Would you feel comfortable renting long term, forgoing ambitions to buy your home and continuing to acquire investment properties?

These questions are sometimes overlooked by rentvestors, who are too often 'sold the dream' by social media campaigns from buyer's agents who aren't taking a long-term view. That said, rentvesting can and does work, and it has certainly enabled plenty of younger Australians to get their foot in the door to purchase where they can afford and live a great lifestyle in an area they want to live in.

Option 3: co-purchase with a sibling or friend

Co-purchasing is another good alternative to consider. If you have a friend or sibling who is willing and able to get into the property market with you, your combined deposits and borrowing capacities could help you to buy a superior property than you could purchase on your own. Another advantage is that it is easier to accumulate a 20 per cent deposit and thus avoid paying fees such as lenders mortgage insurance (LMI). There are also a few lenders who have specific loan products for these scenarios, which can help you manage how you split the loan between you.

Here are some considerations you will need to openly discuss:

- What if you each have different sized deposits?
- What if one person wants to sell in the future and the other person doesn't?
- What if one person meets a partner and wants to buy their next property with them? Will this property need to be sold in order for them to release their cash? Will this property reduce their borrowing capacity to buy their future home?
- What happens if one person is unable to make their loan repayments due to ill health or loss of job?

There are plenty of great examples of co-purchasing being extremely beneficial, so this list of questions should really serve as conversation starters rather than deal-breakers. Going in with transparency and the right legal protections in place can certainly put you in good stead. Having a clear property strategy in place will help align you and your co-purchaser in your intentions and what result you are looking for from this purchase, and clarify the type of property you want and the budget you have to work with.

Option 4: purchase a property that qualifies for first home buyer grants and benefits, then turn it into an investment property

If you are yet to buy a home, it is certainly an option for you to try and maximise any first home buyer grants that could be available to you, depending on which state or territory you live in. You may be able to purchase with only a 5 per cent deposit and not incur LMI, or not pay any stamp duty (or pay a discounted rate). However, factors such as income thresholds and maximum purchase prices may mean that you're not eligible. I don't provide a breakdown of first home buyer grants, discounts or incentives in this book because they vary between different states and territories, and they also change quite regularly.

If you are planning on purchasing your first property and are not intending on living there longer term, then you need to look at this purchase as an investment rather than a home. Here are some of the questions you may want to consider:

- How long am I required to live in this property to be eligible for any first home buyer grants?
- What is the rental potential for this property?
- Will I need to contribute to the loan repayments in the future, or will the rent cover the repayments?
- What will the ongoing costs be for this property as an investment property?
- What work can I do to this property while I am living in it to increase its value and, in turn, generate a higher rental income?

A potential drawback to this option is that you are typically buying based on price to meet grant requirements, and so the property may not be the ideal investment property. For example, if you buy a particular apartment because it's below the maximum purchase price, it may be in a large block, so it doesn't stand out from all the other apartments in the complex and therefore doesn't increase much in value.

Use this line of thinking to help you build out your property strategy when you talk to your mortgage broker about your borrowing capacity. You may also want to consider an interest-only (IO) loan when you convert it to an investment property, which would improve cash flow and also help you save for your own home in the future.

Option 5: consider a sea change or tree change

The exodus from the cities to regional areas during COVID-19 has changed the demographics of so many suburbs. Property prices soared across the country, and freestanding homes commanded a premium. The dream of a sea change or tree change became popular, and it was clear to see why: for the same price as an apartment in a capital city, you could drive an hour or two away and have a larger home close to the water. In New South Wales, the South Coast, Central Coast, North Coast and Blue Mountains regions all witnessed unprecedented increases in property values due to this phenomenon.

From personal experience, you don't want to rush the decision to leave the city and move out to a regional area. It can be different from spending a weekend enjoying the beaches and cafes in the great outdoors. Do your research, spend a few weekends living like a local and perhaps rent in the area to familiarise yourself with your new surroundings before you jump in and buy. If you buy without having spent time in the area, you may be tempted to purchase purely on price, and these properties could be cheaper for a reason. They may get poor sunlight from being on an escarpment side. Perhaps it gets noisy because of peak traffic in the mornings or beachgoers on the weekends in summertime. Spending some time in the area can help you be confident that you will enjoy living your new lifestyle and can buy in a suburb and on a street that you know you will love calling home.

Prior to the birth of our daughter Sienna in 2018, Bernadette and I made a sea change to Thirroul, in the northern suburbs of Wollongong. I'd spent my life in Sydney, whereas Bernadette is originally from the Jervis Bay region further down the South Coast. Thirroul seemed like a happy medium between Sydney and Bernadette's parents, and it allowed us to still be close to the city but far away enough for us to feel like we could enjoy a slower pace of life. Before we moved down, we rented an Airbnb for a weekend to see if we could both see ourselves living there. Once we decided to move down, we then rented for some time to understand the area, get a feel for our new lifestyle and picture ourselves raising a family there. It was certainly an adjustment given that we didn't have a friend network in the area, there wasn't the array of food and dining options that we were accustomed to in Sydney and it was a smaller community. However, it was because of these very things that we started to enjoy our move: we made new friends, explored the area to find new cafes and restaurants and relished building connections with neighbours.

Then, COVID-19 hit literally just as we were ready to purchase, and we saw house prices in the area balloon out of control before our very eyes. We persevered and planned to make a purchase ourselves, but after we struggled to agree on the home we wanted, we engaged a great buyer's agent. We sat down and built our property strategy, which included identifying our non-negotiables, our style of living (we love to entertain and cook), the type of block we wanted and the budget we were working with. We ended up purchasing at auction, and we experienced every emotion a home buyer endures: the frustration of missing out on multiple properties, the disappointment when price guides get blown out the water and the energy of attending Saturday open homes and hoping that this property is 'the one'. The experience gave us a lot of empathy for when we work with home buyers – whether they are purchasing their first home, upgrading their family home or selling up and downsizing with dignity.

Key points

1. Mentally preparing yourself for being a homeowner means you need to shift the way you see yourself, the actions that you need to take and get the right support team around you that can give you the belief and accountability you need to make this dream a reality.

2. There will never be a perfect time to buy. Focus on where you want to buy and what your budget enables you to purchase, and keep saving as much as you can.

3. If you're buying in an area you are unfamiliar with, consider a staycation at a short term rental to get an understanding of the area and where the best pockets are in this suburb. If it's a considerable move, then perhaps a short six-month rental property could be a great way to try before you buy.

Chapter 2

How to save for your deposit

There's a great quote from Greg Reid, author of *The Secret of Happiness*, that goes, 'A dream written down with a date becomes a goal. A goal broken down into steps becomes a plan. A plan backed by actions makes your dreams come true'.

Another saying along these lines is, 'A goal without a plan is just a wish'.

This chapter is all about how to turn your goals into plans so you can work towards saving for your deposit. In chapter 6 I discuss the option of a guarantor loan to expedite the deposit-saving process, but not every home buyer has access to the Bank of Mum and Dad. If this is you, then it's time to roll up your sleeves and start planning. In this chapter, I go through some practical tips that I have worked through with hundreds of clients to help them buy their home.

The odds are stacked against you

To describe the deposit-saving journey any other way than this would be insulting and tone-deaf: the odds are not in your favour. On the flip side, thousands of Australians purchase their first home and get into the property market each year. I'm a great believer that success leaves clues, and if home ownership is the measure of success we're chasing then let's look at the action-takers and see how they have achieved their goal.

It starts with the right mindset. Yes, it will be a testing journey and the goalposts will continue to move. It will feel like an emotional roller-coaster, especially when you see graphs such as figure 2.1, a CoreLogic graph that shows the capital growth in the most recent quarter at the time of writing. However, I need you first to believe that it is achievable and that you are capable of saving for your deposit. As Henry Ford wisely said, 'Whether you think you can or you think you can't, you are right'. Breaking into the Australian property market is hard, so by all means have your pity party, but then get it out of your system and get on with life. Dwelling on the difficulties is not going to help you make any progress; all it will do is build your internal belief that you won't be able to buy your home.

Figure 2.1: capital growth 2023 Q3

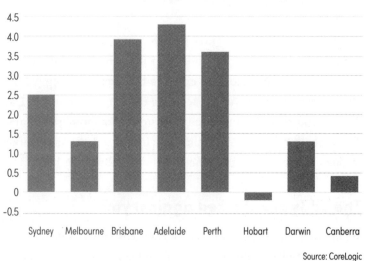

Source: CoreLogic

Using data they commissioned from Resolve Strategic, the *Sydney Morning Herald* published an article in February 2023 titled

'More than 70% of young people believe they'll never be able to buy a home'. According to the research:

- 72 per cent of respondents between the ages of 18 and 34 believe they will never be able to buy a house
- 63 per cent of Australians believe that the young will never be able to buy a home, compared to 57 per cent a year ago
- 49 per cent of renters are renting because they have been priced out of the market (up from 46 per cent the year before), while just 17 per cent have chosen not to buy a house and 27 per cent are confident of buying in the next decade.

Be very careful of the information you absorb; these statistics are somehow 'news' when really they're sentiment and opinion. If you spend your time going down the rabbit hole of how hard it is to buy property, imagine what this does to your subconscious. These reports are intended to stir a reaction, and at the time of writing this article had over 400 comments! What if those people channelled that energy into saving money? This is an illustration of the fact that misery loves company.

It was this article that inspired me to put pen to paper for this book. It lit a fuse in me and made me furious that Australians felt this way. I also realised that I'm in the very privileged position of being able to have some impact on this number. That is my mission in producing this book: to help more Aussies achieve their aspiration to stop renting and buy their home.

No doubt you have friends who complain and moan that they will *never* be able to buy. With that influence around you and the media's rhetoric, it's vital you put yourself in the driver's seat and take control of your perception – and so I applaud you for reading this book. The mere act of feeding your mind can be the game changer that allows you to proudly buy your own home. Just consider for a moment that in the history of home-buying in Australia, millions of people have achieved this. You're not the first to aspire to this, nor will you be the last to succeed.

Now you've got your head in the game, you need a strategy and clear next steps to keep you on track. Here are three steps to take when beginning your savings journey.

Step 1: review your income and expenses

A common misconception is that you need to begin by creating a budget. While having a budget is helpful, it's not the best place to start. First, you need to look under the hood of your transaction account and calculate how much is coming in, how much is going out and how much is left over. Don't be tempted to start downloading apps or spend-tracking software, though; I love technology and how much it can help and automate our finances but this is something that requires you to grab a pen and paper and do the work yourself. The act of putting pen to paper makes this a 'write to learn' activity, which is an effective way to learn through engagement as it's more active. You can download a template from happyhomeloanbook.com.au.

The goal of this exercise is to know your numbers. If you are telling yourself *I'm not good with numbers*, I'm sorry but that's a cop-out excuse; you absolutely need to know your budget. Imagine a business owner who didn't know their revenue, expenses and profit numbers – they do exist, but they don't last long in business.

You need to dig up expenses that are paid weekly, such as public transport and petrol; monthly, such as subscriptions, tele-communications services and memberships; and annually, such as car insurance and home and contents insurance. Complexity is the enemy here, so just write down all the expenses that you see being direct-debited from your transaction account.

I recall when Bernadette and I did this exercise, we were shocked at how many direct debits were flying under the radar. We thought we were diligent with our expenses, yet some payments had crept in there, such as digital subscriptions, and it can take quite a bit of effort to cancel them. The result for us was crystal clear: we knew exactly how much was coming in and how much it cost for us to live, and the number frightened us! We don't live a lavish lifestyle, and yet the difference between our income and expenses was slim. We had a discussion about the non-negotiables in our lives and what could be cut and took the view that every single dollar we spent had to be justified. This can feel like it takes the enjoyment out of life, but we had a clear goal in mind to buy our home and we knew we had to make some sacrifices along the way.

Once you have made as many cuts to your expenses as possible, you should be left with three key numbers:

1. your income
2. your expenses
3. your savings.

Step 2: set up your 'Spending', 'Safety' and 'My Home Deposit' accounts

Your employer pays your salary, the government receives your tax, you pay your bills and then you save whatever is left over. Right? Unfortunately, this equation won't work for you moving forward. You need to pay yourself first, and then you have to live off the rest. I've mentioned making sacrifices already, and you're on a mission to buy a home here, so let's get serious about it. (If you're already diligently working towards your savings target, I applaud you and encourage you to keep going.)

This step involves making changes to the way your banking is set up. Nickname your daily account 'Spending' and your emergency funds account 'Safety', then set up a new savings account and nickname this 'My Home Deposit'. (It's important to keep your 'My Home Deposit' account separate from your 'Safety' account so that you have the cash if an emergency or a surprise bill comes up.) This will reinforce that you are on a mission and keep you accountable to achieving your savings target. You could also go one step further and ask your employer to amend the way you are paid – some employment payroll platforms may allow you to make this change yourself – and elect for a specific amount to be paid into the 'My Home Deposit' account and the remainder into your everyday transaction account where all your expenses come from. This change makes saving non-negotiable.

Bernadette and I adopted this philosophy in our household. The discipline of managing our money across three separate bank accounts made all the difference for us.

Step 3: know your savings target

This is where the rubber hits the road for you and you start taking steps to turn your dreams into reality. You need to know your destination and how you're going to get there. Get in touch with a mortgage broker and explain that you are trying to work out your borrowing capacity. By having an idea of how much a bank will lend you, you can start to get an idea of what type of property you want to purchase and an estimate of how much it would cost. The idea here is to then work backwards to figure out the associated costs:

Purchase price (an estimate is fine)	_____
Stamp duty (if applicable)	_____
Legal fees (an estimate is fine)	$2000
Additional costs (settlement fees)	$500

How much deposit do you need to save, depending on how much you think you can contribute?

20% = _____

15% = _____

10% = _____

5% = _____

Total I need to save to buy my home _____

Now that you know how much you need to save, you can work out how long it will take. Divide the total savings required by monthly savings target to calculate how many months it will take you to save to buy your home. This is the magic number, the focal point for your savings. Write it down and stick it on your bathroom mirror or car vanity mirror, or make it your phone wallpaper or computer desktop background. Seeing this daily will reinforce your goal.

Become an elite savings athlete

There are no shortcuts in this journey – you need to be disciplined, focused and accountable.

I once enrolled in a corporate boxing challenge. This was a 12-week intensive program that involved a rigorous training regime to prepare me for a fight at the end of the program. Every training session mattered, but this was only one part of the winning equation. I needed the right trainer and the right gear. My diet had to reflect a boxer's diet, which meant being organised with my meal preparation. I also needed to have the right mindset and picture myself winning. This visualisation technique is critical; there is significant scientific evidence that shows our brains can't differentiate between what we visualise and reality, so visualising your goal teaches your brain to believe that it can be a reality. Powerful, isn't it? And most importantly, I needed the right support network that could reinforce my winning mindset.

I won my fight, but there's no ego in that. I needed to stack the odds in my favour and do everything within my power to prepare to make sure I could achieve this outcome. The moral of my story is that success is the sum of its parts; one part in isolation isn't enough to get you the win.

I encourage and challenge you to look at everything in your life that can help you succeed in saving for your deposit. I believe there is no greater goal you can work towards in life than aiming to buy your own home.

Key points

1. You're going to need to shut off all the external noise about how hard it is to save for your deposit. You can do it.

2. The three keys to saving for your deposit are reviewing your income and expenses; setting up your 'Spending', 'Safety' and 'My Home Deposit' bank accounts; and knowing your savings target.

3. Write down your savings target on a piece of paper and stick it wherever you will see it regularly. Seeing it regularly will reinforce your goal.

Chapter 3

Understanding your borrowing capacity

As a mortgage broker, the question I get asked most often is 'How much can I borrow?' The goal of this chapter is to take you into my world and explain the nuances of how different lenders calculate your borrowing capacity. There are several variables that can influence your borrowing capacity, so let's explore them in more detail.

Income

The best place to start is with your income. If you are on a salary, your borrowing capacity is calculated using your gross annual income. Depending on the industry you work in and your role, your borrowing capacity may also be affected by additional income sources:

- **Bonus income.** As a general rule of thumb, lenders want to see the last two years of bonus payments with your current employer, though some may consider one year's bonus. Some lenders will use your most recent year's bonus in their borrowing capacity calculation while other lenders may average the two years, and others still may take the lowest bonus payment. If your salary package has a large bonus component, it's best to pull together a summary of your payments to determine which lender would be a suitable fit for your situation.

- **Commissions.** Many sales roles have a commission element to their remuneration. Similar to bonus payments, most lenders want evidence of your last two years of commission payments. I often hear about future commissions that are coming, but lenders won't accept payments until they have actually hit your bank account.
- **Allowances.** In some industries such as hospitality, medical and emergency services, allowances or penalty rates are paid. Some lenders can include 100 per cent of your allowances or penalty rates in their assessment of your borrowing capacity.
- **Tax-free income.** Most lenders will accept Parts A and B of the Family Tax Benefit, especially if your children are under 11. When it comes to other government payments such as the carer allowance, lenders look at these on a case-by-case basis.
- **Second job income.** If you have another role on the side, perhaps the Army Reserve or a casual job, it's best to provide as much information about this as possible to work out which lenders will include this in their assessment. The catch with casual income is that lenders want to see your work history over the last six months.
- **Rental income.** If you have an investment property, most lenders will use 80 per cent of the weekly rental income in their calculations.

What if I'm self-employed?

In the past, banks had a reputation for being inflexible with self-employed clients, but the times have changed and many lenders now have brilliant policies around this. For example, if you have been paying yourself a consistent salary for six months and you can provide confirmation through payslips and corresponding payments into your bank account, they will use this income just as if you were a salaried employee.

Some lenders will work off your last notice of assessment (NOA), whereas others will want you to provide two years' worth of company and individual tax returns. There is no one-size-fits-all policy with self-employed income. If you are willing to seek out an expert mortgage broker, they will be worth their weight in gold, providing you with options you would not traditionally get by going directly to one bank.

Expenses

I feel that the days of lenders looking through your bank statements like investigators at a crime scene are behind us, thanks largely to the rise of more efficient technology tools like bankstatements.com.au. However, it's certainly important for you to know your outgoings to manage your personal budget:

- **Living expenses.** This is a monthly number that reflects your day-to-day outgoings, such as subscriptions, gym memberships and travel expenses. Living expenses are benchmarked under a method called the Household Expenditure Measure (HEM). In addition to this monthly number, some lenders may also add on your private health insurance fees and children's private school fees. It's also helpful for you to know that different lenders will work off slightly different HEMs, which can influence your final borrowing capacity.
- **Credit cards.** Banks will consider the *limit* on your credit card as a liability, irrespective of your balance or if you rarely use it.

The logic is quite reasonable – you could max out your credit card tomorrow. The impact of credit cards on your borrowing capacity is significant, and it never ceases to amaze me how many of my clients place a higher importance on keeping a credit card than cutting it to improve or increase their borrowing capacity.

- **Personal or car loans.** These types of loans will significantly reduce your borrowing capacity. In my experience, it often helps to pay out these loans to increase your borrowing capacity. This can leave you with a slightly lower deposit, but you have options to consider to mitigate this, such as lenders mortgage insurance (LMI), which we'll discuss in more detail in chapter 5.
- **Salary sacrifices or car leases.** While these may be tax-effective options, they will drag down your borrowing capacity. Consider if they can be paid out to improve your borrowing capacity.
- **HECS-HELP debt.** Look at your payslip and see how much you're paying off your HECS-HELP loan on a regular basis. This repayment amount will be factored into your borrowing capacity. The balance of your overall debt will impact how much you can borrow, too, so it's worth jumping online and finding this out.
- **Associated costs with owning an investment property.** Along with shaving off 20 per cent of your weekly rental income, some lenders will also want to include all the outgoing expenses related to owning your investment property. These may include strata fees, property management expenses and utility bills.

You might be picking up a vibe that I'm all about finding ways to *improve* your borrowing capacity. Please don't misinterpret this as me trying to load you up with more debt. I take the view that improving your borrowing capacity is all about allowing you to afford a superior property without having to compromise on key attributes of your home, such as avoiding buying on a main street or with a south-facing aspect. I unpack this in more detail in chapter 9 as we talk about how to identify a high-quality property.

Assessment rate

The assessment rate is commonly referred to as the lender's 'stress test' rate. The lender will add 2 to 3 per cent on top of the actual interest rate of your loan; this buffer allows for interest-rate rises from the RBA.

The big four banks (ANZ, Commonwealth Bank of Australia, National Australia Bank and Westpac), along with second-tier lenders (such as Macquarie Bank, ING, Suncorp, Bankwest and AMP) and credit unions and building societies (such as Teachers Mutual Bank and Newcastle Permanent), all fall under the regulation of the Australian Prudential Regulation Authority (APRA). When APRA recommends 3 per cent as the loan serviceability buffer, for example, these lenders will need to heed their guidance.

These lenders are also covered under the Financial Claims Scheme (FCS), which is why most borrowers will typically feel 'safer' when they apply through these lenders. For a full list of lenders covered by the FCS, check out apra.gov.au/list-of-authorised-deposit-taking-institutions-covered-under-financial-claims-scheme.

Non-bank lenders are great alternatives to consider as they don't have as many restrictions placed on them by APRA. This can sometimes lead to them being mischaracterised as riskier, but in reality they have to comply with all the same legislation as the lenders that are regulated by APRA. Non-bank lenders have some flexibility in their policies, such as taking 100 per cent of rental income rather than 80 per cent. Being leaner and more nimble means that they can lend in 'greyer' situations.

Because of the flexibility they offer, their interest rate sometimes comes at a premium. Don't let this deter you, though – they offer a brilliant way to get into the property market. Also, if you can maintain a great repayment history for three to six months, then you can look into options to refinance your loan with a mainstream lender at a lower interest rate.

Credit score

A giant myth when it comes to getting a home loan approved is that you need a great credit score. Not true – you just need to ensure you don't have previous credit issues, such as missed payments. Along with this misconception is the fallacy that you need to apply for a credit card to have a credit score. Let's clear this up – getting and using a credit card to improve your 'creditworthiness' sounds like a great marketing campaign launched by a bank many moons ago. Perhaps it comes from the United States, where they rely heavily on their Fair, Isaac and Company (FICO®) scoring model.

Your credit score is calculated using various metrics, which are summarised in your credit report. This information includes:

- how often you have applied for credit products
- what current liabilities you have in place
- your repayment history on your loans or credit cards
- whether you have any missed repayments, defaults, court judgements or bankruptcies.

Credit scores differ between providers. The classifications of the main credit reporting bodies are outlined in table 3.1.

There are a number of 'free' credit report websites you can access. From experience, these are good but not great. At Atelier Wealth, we run a complimentary credit report before your loan is submitted to ensure we don't encounter potential issues. This doesn't register as a credit enquiry. If you would like a credit report ordered for you, please get in contact.

Table 3.1: credit-score classifications of the main
credit reporting bodies

Credit score range	illion	Equifax	Experian
Excellent	800–1000	833–1200	800–1000
Very good	700–799	726–832	700–799
Average	500–699	622–725	625–699
Fair	300–499	510–621	550–624
Low	0–299	0–509	0–549

How your borrowing capacity can vary from bank to bank

We've all seen the advertisements for Industry SuperFunds that 'compare the pair', showing how the superannuation fund performance of two people of the same age, income and starting balance can vary over time. I think of this ad every time I try to explain borrowing capacity. All the variables I've discussed in this chapter can lead you to different borrowing capacities, depending on what variables apply to you and which path you take.

This section shows you how things can vary when it comes time to do the number crunching for your borrowing capacity. As I've mentioned, lenders' assessment rates and HEMs will vary and thus produce different results.

Scenario one assesses a solo borrower earning $100,000 per annum and compares their borrowing capacity with or without a $10,000 credit card (see table 3.2, overleaf).

The core message I'm trying to share with you is that your property purchase decision is influenced by how much you can borrow. Can you imagine if you only went to Lender X, and you had no idea they gave you the lowest borrowing capacity and you had the ability to comfortably borrow more?

Table 3.2: borrowing capacity of a solo borrower earning $100,000 p.a.

	Max. capacity with credit card	Max. capacity without credit card
Lender 1	$478,924	$528,390
Lender 2	$486,381	$528,191
Lender 3	$464,582	$508,489
Lender 4	$451,359	$498,250
Lender 5	$449,084	$495,726
Lender 6	$447,765	$493,753
Lender 7	$446,616	$493,052
Lender 8	$446,282	$492,950
Lender 9	$446,309	$492,663
Lender 10	$444,346	$490,496
Lender 11	$444,266	$490,457
Lender 12	$439,723	$485,390
Lender 13	$439,321	$484,948
Lender 14	$437,521	$483,148
Lender 15	$437,418	$482,846
Lender 16	$437,171	$437,171

Scenario two assesses a couple with a combined annual income of $180,000 and compares their borrowing capacity with or without a $20,000 credit card (see table 3.3).

Table 3.3: borrowing capacity of a couple earning
a combined $180,000 p.a.

	Max. capacity with credit card	Max. capacity without credit card
Lender 1	$866,864	$950,485
Lender 2	$841,668	$940,600
Lender 3	$818,491	$906,307
Lender 4	$793,182	$886,964
Lender 5	$792,864	$884,118
Lender 6	$789,030	$882,314
Lender 7	$785,658	$877,634
Lender 8	$784,277	$877,615
Lender 9	$784,564	$877,436
Lender 10	$784,094	$876,802
Lender 11	$780,768	$873,149
Lender 12	$780,645	$872,945
Lender 13	$772,490	$864,547
Lender 14	$772,611	$863,945
Lender 15	$771,869	$863,123
Lender 16	$768,518	$859,374

Scenario three assesses the same couple from scenario two, without a credit card, but this time it compares their borrowing capacity with or without a baby (see table 3.4, overleaf) – the banks lovingly call this blessing a 'dependant'.

You can see in scenario three the impact that a baby can have on your borrowing capacity. I have used the same gross income, but in my experience one parent usually returns to work part-time, which would push down their household time and, in turn, reduce their borrowing capacity even further.

Table 3.4: borrowing capacity of a couple earning a combined $180,000 p.a. with or without a dependant

	Max. capacity without dependant	Max. capacity with dependant
Lender 1	$950,485	$904,186
Lender 2	$940,600	$890,258
Lender 3	$906,307	$859,665
Lender 4	$886,964	$840,566
Lender 5	$884,118	$838,999
Lender 6	$882,314	$836,216
Lender 7	$877,615	$831,717
Lender 8	$877,436	$831,489
Lender 9	$877,634	$831,418
Lender 10	$876,802	$830,935
Lender 11	$873,149	$827,444
Lender 12	$872,945	$827,281
Lender 13	$864,547	$819,056
Lender 14	$863,945	$818,759
Lender 15	$863,123	$818,028
Lender 16	$859,374	$814,474

This type of scenario becomes incredibly important when I'm having conversations with clients who want to buy their home and are also thinking about starting a family. Do you purchase before your baby arrives or afterwards, knowing that your income and, in turn, your borrowing capacity will decrease? Your answer to this question will depend on your unique journey and priorities. Do you value the stability and security of owning your home and nesting before the baby arrives? Do you fear having to make repayments on your home loan while being down to one income during maternity leave? These are normal and natural concerns, which is why running the numbers on these scenarios allows you to make smart money and property decisions.

Key points

1. Every lender will give you a different borrowing capacity outcome; explore your options.
2. Spend some time reviewing your income and expenses, and pull together a summary to share with your mortgage broker.
3. Understand the impact your current loans have on your borrowing capacity and be open to closing them to improve your loan serviceability.

Chapter 4

Loans, explained

In this chapter, I give you a detailed breakdown of the different types of loans, structures and repayment types, and how interest rates can vary depending on the loan you choose. I hope this becomes a key reference point for you to demystify home loans and make you more confident when discussing your loan structure options with your mortgage broker.

Loan terms

The term of the loan refers to how long you have to pay off your loan. The standard home loan term is 30 years, though there are a few lenders who offer 35- or 40-year loan terms.

Some Australians want to pay off their home loan as quickly as possible – say, in 15 years. If this is you, it's ideal to start with a standard 30-year loan and then calculate your repayments to be in line with your 15-year target, rather than initially applying for a 15-year loan term. If you do initially apply for a 15-year loan term rather than a 30-year loan term, your borrowing capacity will be reduced because you will be assessed on your ability to service your loan in a 15-year period. In addition, you won't be able to extend your loan term back out to 30 years unless you go through the process of reapplying for a 30-year loan term. Starting out with a 30-year loan term gives you some flexibility; for example, if you have children and are down to one income for a while, or if you're temporarily out of work, you have the option to revert to your minimum repayments rather than being stuck at the higher 15-year repayment rate.

Repayment types

There are two loan repayment types: principal and interest (P&I) and interest-only (IO).

Principal and interest repayments

P&I repayments are the most common type. With this loan repayment type, borrowers choose to actively pay down their 'principal', which is the amount of money they originally borrowed from the lender. The 'interest' component is the cost that the lender charges you for borrowing this money, and the amount of interest is determined by your interest rate. The most significant benefit of a P&I loan repayment is that your repayments reduce over time as you keep paying down your principal loan amount.

Figure 4.1 (overleaf) shows how much of your repayment of a 30-year loan is interest rather than principal. Over time, as your principal slowly decreases, the amount of interest you pay comes down. By actively making additional repayments, you reduce your loan term, which reduces how much interest you pay over the life of your loan. Figure 4.2 (overleaf) provides the comparison of a 15-year loan term to show how much interest you can save.

If your P&I loan is structured with an offset account (which it should be), it's important to understand how this helps with your repayments. An offset account is a normal savings account that is linked to your home loan. You can have multiple offset accounts linked to your home loan, which is especially useful if you manage your cash flow using the buckets methodology made famous by Scott Pape in *The Barefoot Investor*.

Figure 4.1: P&I repayments over a 30-year loan term

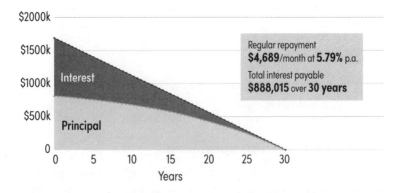

Figure 4.2: P&I repayments over a 15-year loan term

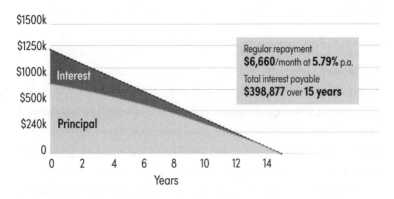

Source: https://atelierwealth.com.au/calculators/repayment

Let's walk through an example of how a linked offset account can affect your P&I repayments (see table 4.1). With a balance of $50,000 in your offset account, your monthly repayment is still the same, but a greater proportion of that payment goes towards repaying the principal.

Table 4.1: example of P&I loan repayments with and without an offset account

Offset account amount	$0 (no offset account)	$50,000
Loan balance	$800,000	$800,000
Interest rate	5.79%	5.79%
Monthly repayment: principal	$820	$1070
Monthly repayment: interest	$3860	$3619
Monthly repayment: total	$4689	$4689

In this example, you are making an additional $250 in principal repayments per month by having $50,000 in your linked offset account.

Interest-only repayments

IO loans are less favoured by homeowners as you are not actively paying down your home loan, only the interest component. An IO loan term is usually a maximum of five years, after which it reverts to a P&I loan repayment unless you reapply for an IO loan, which requires resubmitting your documents and information (and most likely refinancing with another lender).

The main benefit of an IO loan is that repayments are lower than with a P&I loan, which can assist with your cash flow. For example, if you are going on parental leave and will be down to one income for a while, making the switch to IO repayments could tide you over during that period, especially if you will be receiving limited financial support from the government or your employer.

Other reasons to discuss IO repayments with your mortgage broker include if you intend to sell the home in a few years or you want to undertake renovations. In these scenarios, the strategy could be to put as much cash as possible into your offset account. The more cash you hold in your offset account, the more your monthly repayment is reduced (see table 4.2).

Table 4.2: example of IO loan repayments with and without an offset account

Offset account amount	$0 (no offset account)	$50,000
Loan balance (effective)	$800,000	$750,000
Interest rate	6.15%	6.15%
Monthly repayment	$4100	$3844

Something to take into consideration with an IO loan is that your interest rate will most likely be higher than with a P&I loan. Lenders add a 'loading' onto the interest rate for all IO loan products. You also need to be aware that IO loan repayments are set to monthly, so you cannot opt for weekly or fortnightly repayments under an IO loan. Some lenders may not allow you to elect for IO repayments if your loan-to-value ratio (LVR) is greater than 90 per cent (that is, if the value of your loan is more than 90 per cent of the total value of the property), so it's worth discussing this with your mortgage broker.

Another thing to discuss with your mortgage broker is whether opting for IO repayments will impact your borrowing capacity. The reason for this is that lenders assess your serviceability over the P&I loan term, so if you choose to go IO for five years out of a 30-year loan, you will need to service your home loan over a 25-year period, which, given it is a shorter loan term, will decrease your borrowing capacity.

Should your loan be variable, fixed or split?

Another consideration when choosing a home loan is how the interest rate is set. There are three broad options: variable, fixed and split.

Variable-rate home loans

With a variable-rate home loan, your regular interest repayments will fluctuate in line with the RBA's cash rate and, in turn, how your lender passes on these rate changes. Some countries refer to this type of loan as 'floating' or 'adjustable'. These fluctuations come with the obvious disadvantage of uncertainty, but a benefit of variable-rate loans is the ability they provide to make extra repayments without any penalties, which ultimately helps you to pay off your loan faster. They also tend to come with an offset account feature.

Fixed-rate home loans

If you are looking for consistent repayments to help with your budgeting and want certainty that your interest rate will not fluctuate, then a fixed-rate home loan may suit you. It's also a helpful option if you feel that interest rates may increase; by fixing your interest rate today, you are protected against future rate increases for the duration of your fixed-rate loan term.

In Australia, fixed-rate loans generally have a maximum period of five years. You may have heard that some other countries, such as the United States, offer 30-year fixed-rate loans. There is a stark difference between these two countries' mortgage regulations. The biggest distinction is that the US has government-sponsored enterprises (GSEs) that purchase mortgages from lenders, whereas Australia does not.

In general, fixed-rate loans do not come with an offset account option, though there are a handful of lenders that have a fixed-rate loan product with an offset account. Also, fixed-rate loans cap how much extra you are able to pay off your loan. Some lenders will allow you to make additional repayments up to a certain figure (say, $10,000 or $20,000) per financial year of your fixed-rate loan, while other lenders will have a percentage limit. This means that if you receive large lump-sum payments such as commissions or bonuses, you are limited in how much you can use these to pay down your loan. It's also important to note that if you don't hit the annual additional repayment limit, the remaining balance does not roll over to the next financial year.

Another consideration when you choose a fixed-rate loan is that in exchange for a 'rate lock fee', your lender will guarantee that the interest rate of the fixed-rate loan will not change between when you apply for your loan and when you settle on a property. Yes, this is a real thing, and while I particularly hate it, it is an option for you. Some lenders will charge you a flat fee, such as $750, while other lenders will charge you a percentage of the loan amount. Your rate lock with most lenders is valid for 90 days, so if you are applying for pre-approval then it could become a sunk cost if you don't find your home within this period. If you choose not to pay it, then you run the risk of interest rates increasing by the time you settle and getting stuck with a higher interest rate than you anticipated.

If you are considering fixing the interest rate on your home loan for up to five years, you need to factor in whether you anticipate any major changes to your situation occurring during this period. If your circumstances change during your fixed-rate period and you need to pay out your loan, you could incur a break fee, which the lender calculates using an algorithm. If you need to sell and move houses, you have the option to switch out the 'security' – that is, to switch the property that is linked to the loan with the home you are purchasing. This is known as 'security substitution' or 'loan portability', and it also incurs a fee.

Split home loans: the best of both worlds

Another option is to fix part of your home loan and keep the rest variable. If you are unsure what percentage of your loan to fix, you are not alone – this is a commonly asked question. To help you work out your options, I have created a calculator that you can plug the interest rates for the variable and fixed portions of the loan into, which you can access at atelierwealth.com.au/downloadables/. You can then play around with the loan amounts and fixed/variable proportions to estimate your monthly repayments in various scenarios. There is no set percentage you need to have fixed and variable; it really depends on your situation. Here are some factors to consider when making this decision:

- How much extra can you save each month to utilise the benefit of an offset account?
- How much extra do you think you want to make in additional repayments?
- What does your research tell you about interest-rate movements over the next few years? How much do you anticipate your variable repayments will fluctuate? Will the fixed rate protect you against rising rates or hinder you if rates come down?

Chat with your mortgage broker about options to split your loan and use the calculator tool to help you work out the sweet spot between how much of your loan you would like to be fixed versus variable.

Other considerations

We've now covered the main things to consider when choosing how to structure your home loan, but there are some other factors and loan types that may be relevant to your situation.

Basic versus packaged loans

Basic home loans, as the name implies, are a no-frills loan product. They come with no annual fee or offset account. You do get a redraw functionality, but this is pretty standard across all loan products. While a basic home loan may seem like an attractive option as it usually comes with a low interest rate, my suggestion is not to be tempted. Lenders dangle these low-rate products, but why would you want your loan to be 'basic'?

The alternative is a 'packaged' loan, which gives you a discount off the standard variable interest rate and access to offset accounts and other products, such as credit cards and discounted insurance products. Yes, a packaged loan requires you to pay an annual fee, but your future self will thank you for the extra benefits. Too many people start with a basic loan because they are cheaper, but lenders will not review the rates and provide discounts for loyalty, which usually means people outgrow a basic loan and transition to a packaged loan.

Introductory loans

Introductory loans have a low interest rate to attract borrowers. Also known as a 'honeymoon' rate, it generally only lasts for around 12 months before rising to standard rates. Rates can be fixed or capped.

Lines of credit

You may have heard the term 'lines of credit'. Though a line of credit is not always applicable at the start of your home-buying journey, it can be a helpful tool down the track. The easiest way to explain a line of credit is that it is similar to a credit card with a master limit that is secured against your home. When your home value increases and makes equity available, if you have the borrowing capacity, you could choose to apply for a line of credit. This is a separate loan account, which is usually IO and which you can use for investments such as shares or, potentially, a deposit on an investment property.

Low-doc loans

If you are self-employed or your situation is a little unconventional, you might consider a low-documentation (low-doc) loan, which has fewer requirements you need to fulfil to have the loan approved. There are specialist lenders that play in this niche quite well. Perhaps your business has turned a corner and you've had a great few quarters of sales results and profitability. Rather than waiting for the end of the financial year, some lenders will work with your accountant and use your business activity statements (BAS) or an accountant declaration to approve your loan. It's important to engage your accountant as early as possible to ensure they are on board and have options to help you, as not all accountants are able or willing to provide a declaration to a lender. The price to pay for this level of lender flexibility is a higher interest rate and perhaps some additional fees, depending on your LVR and loan amount.

Bridging loans

If you have fallen in love with a property and want to buy it but have not yet sold your current home, a bridging loan may be able to help you. A bridging loan is a short-term loan that gives you a brief window (say, six months) to finance your purchase while you go through the process of selling your home. There are a handful of lenders that offer bridging loans and their policies differ. If you are actively looking for a property and you haven't got the ball rolling on listing and selling your home, you need to engage your broker early as you do not want to rush this process. Some lenders may charge higher interest rates for bridging loans, so you need to have your eyes wide open and carefully consider the different bridging loan options and how long you need the loan for.

Construction loans

If you have purchased a vacant block of land and will be building your home, you will need a construction loan to finance the construction of the property. Once you have settled on your land loan and your builder is ready to commence construction, your lender will make 'progress payments' to your builder when they hit certain build milestones – for example, 20 per cent when they lay the slab, 20 per cent when they complete the frame, 20 per cent at lock-up, 20 per cent at fit-out and the final 20 per cent upon completion. As these progress payments are made, your total loan amount gradually increases. Once construction has been completed, the loan is fully drawn down.

How often should I make repayments on my loan?

There is a debate that rages over the most efficient repayment period for paying off your loan as quickly as possible – weekly, fortnightly or monthly? In reality, the most important factor for paying off your loan as quickly as possible is to make additional repayments as often as you can and put as much cash as possible into your offset account. These two actions will far outweigh the impact of trying to chase the most efficient repayment rate. With that said, however, let's explore the difference between different repayment frequencies:

- **Monthly** is the most common frequency and often the default setting for lenders, so this is likely what you'll end up with if you don't specifically elect a different option. If your loan is split or variable, some lenders offer you the option to choose your repayment date so you can line it up with your pay cycle; this option may not be available if your loan is fixed.
- **Fortnightly** is considered ideal as you make 26 payments a year, which is like making an extra month's repayment. It's important

to check that your lender offers 'true' fortnightly repayments, though, as some banks have been known to work out your annual repayments and divide by 26 (rather than simply halving the monthly repayment amount), which doesn't give you an advantage.

- **Weekly** is more favourable if you manage your budget on a weekly basis, but it doesn't give you a significant advantage over fortnightly repayments.

Table 4.3 compares monthly, fortnightly and weekly repayments on an $800,000 loan at an interest rate of 6%.

Table 4.3: monthly versus fortnightly versus weekly repayments

Repayment period	Monthly	Fortnightly	Weekly
Repayment amount	$4796.40	$2398.20	$1199.10
Total interest paid	$926,706	$728,209	$727,329
Total interest saved	$0	$198,497	$199,377
Time saved	0 years, 0 months	5 years, 6 months	5 years, 6 months

The difference between fortnightly and weekly repayments is very small, but either option is much better than making the minimum monthly repayments.

Discuss your loan strategy with your mortgage broker

Yes, I'm biased to suggest going to a mortgage broker given that I am a mortgage broker myself. Pause for a moment, though, and think of all the times you've sought a second opinion on a big purchase.

Whether it's a $2000 laptop, a $10,000 holiday or a $30,000 car, you would never accept just one option, so why would you simply ask one lender for their policies and interest rates without comparing and competing? We're talking about your home loan here – it pays to shop around. Your borrowing capacity will vary from lender to lender and, depending on your income and expenses, this could mean a significant difference in the type of property you can afford to purchase.

This is why it's important to have a 'loan strategy'. It's about more than just ensuring your loan comes with an offset account; it's really about how your loan is structured and making sure it aligns with your future property ambitions. For example, if you're planning to turn this property into an investment once you move out of it then you might choose an IO loan, whereas if you are buying a home for the long term and want to actively pay down your loan with additional repayments then you would likely opt for a P&I or split loan with a variable rate.

Another critical element of your loan strategy is knowing your absolute 'stretch' purchase price. This is vital if you are going to be bidding at an auction – you would hate to miss out over a few thousand dollars because you didn't realise you could nudge your purchase price higher, whether that means increasing your deposit or paying a bit of LMI.

Determining your loan strategy is crucial for getting your pre-approval organised (which I discuss further in chapter 8). There is absolutely no harm in being prepared with your pre-approval given it can be valid for three to six months with most lenders. During this three- to six-month time period, though, you can experience life changes; here are some of the most common:

- You change roles, whether to a new job with a probation period or to become a contractor. This may invalidate your pre-approval with the lender you have chosen.

- Your deposit has decreased due to a holiday or a new car purchase (which I do not recommend at this stage), and your purchase price was reliant upon having a certain deposit amount.
- You take on a personal loan, a new credit card or buy now pay later (BPNL) facility, which limits your borrowing capacity.
- You have a baby and go on maternity leave. (Congratulations!) You are now down to one income and have a dependent child, which will decrease your borrowing capacity.

These are not uncommon scenarios, but it is absolutely critical if any major life event arises that you contact your mortgage broker to discuss the implications. Some of the examples I've mentioned may not be deal-breakers, but being prepared will ensure your broker can stay proactive and revise your numbers rather than trying to calculate this once you have found the property you want to buy.

Key points

1. Take the time to work through your loan structure options with your mortgage broker. This part of the process is far too often overlooked, and questions come up only after the loan settles. Slow down to speed up – that's the name of the loan application game.

2. If you are unsure of the jargon being used, feel free to ask for terms to be translated into plain English. If you're going to sign off on your loan application and other documentation, please take note of what you are signing.

3. There is no one-size-fits-all approach; the loan that suits your friends or family may not be the most suitable for you. Overlook the lowest interest rate and find the solution that caters to your situation best.

Chapter 5

Lenders mortgage insurance – friend or foe?

I love Scott Pape, the Barefoot Investor. He's done an incredible job of raising the standard of financial literacy across Australia. We use the bucket system in our household – Bernadette deserves the credit for this; I would just keep spending! – and it works. But I need to politely disagree with one piece of his advice, which is having to save a 20 per cent deposit to buy your home. I'm sorry, Scotty, but this is just not possible for everyone, and as they continue to save diligently the Australian property market is outpacing their ability to save. In my mind, I can conjure up responses to the rebuttals I imagine Mr Pape would offer.

Rebuttal 1: buy a cheaper home in a cheaper area

This is a very reasonable option to consider. However, having to move further away from friends and family can mean a seismic shift in your social life. It can also mean a longer commute time, leaving earlier and getting home later, and therefore spending less time with your family. I've seen this play out, and it can sometimes lead to resentment that you have a home but have to spend less time in it and more time travelling.

Rebuttal 2: cut out as much from your spending as possible so you can keep saving until you have a 20 per cent deposit

I absolutely agree that cutting as much as possible from your spending is critical to reaching the goal of home ownership. Every home buyer has made some sacrifices to achieve their dream of buying their own home, whether through giving up holidays, forgoing a new car purchase or making small sacrifices such as making lunch and not buying coffee out – whatever it takes. But the Sydney property market, as an example, is growing at 6 per cent year on year; this is called 'capital growth', and as it compounds it moves the horizon further and further away.

Rebuttal 3: lenders mortgage insurance (LMI) is a total waste of money

LMI is a fee, and we all hate incurring unnecessary fees, but LMI could be necessary if you want to get into the market sooner rather than later. Let's look into the reality of saving for a 20 per cent deposit versus saving the minimum and paying LMI.

Imagine you are saving to buy an $800,000 home in Sydney. The median annual income in Sydney is $94,130. If you are single, this would mean your monthly net income is $5929. If you live in a unit, median rent would cost $2900 per month. If you pay for the basics according to the HEM benchmark, that works out to $1100 per month. This leaves you with $1929 left over each month to put into savings. At this rate, to save $160,000 for a 20 per cent deposit would take you 83 months, or nearly seven years. That's insane!

Table 5.1 (overleaf) compares this rate of saving to the rate of capital growth an $800,000 property would experience over seven years at 6 per cent.

By year seven, you have diligently saved $162,036 (a little over your $160,000 target), but rising prices mean you now need a deposit of almost $227,000 to buy your home. You also need $45,805 in stamp duty now, because the value of the property has exceeded the first home buyer stamp duty concession threshold. This means you now need $272,768, which means you're short by $110,732.

Table 5.1: saving for a 20 per cent deposit on an $800,000 property in Sydney

Year	Amount saved	Property value	Amount required for a 20% deposit
1	$23,148	$800,000	$160,000
2	$46,296	$848,000	$169,600
3	$69,444	$898,880	$179,776
4	$92,592	$952,813	$190,563
5	$115,740	$1,009,982	$201,996
6	$138,888	$1,070,580	$214,116
7	$162,036	$1,134,815	$226,963

Now let's compare this scenario to saving the minimum deposit you need to purchase this property (5 per cent) and paying LMI. In 30 months (two and a half years), you will have saved $57,870. The value of this property is now $873,000, which means the stamp duty payable is $14,503. Your savings minus the stamp duty payable is $43,367. The 5 per cent minimum deposit is $43,650, which leaves you short by $283, which I'm sure you could save.

Doesn't this target of 30 months rather than seven years give you the confidence to realise that home ownership could be closer than you thought? My view is that the tone-deaf statement of having to save a 20 per cent deposit is unrealistic, unmotivating and lacks empathy. The property market has rapidly changed post-COVID-19, and if you are caught in the rental trap, all this statement is doing is pushing back your dreams of buying your home into oblivion.

If you can see yourself buying your home and setting a target to save and buy, then perhaps reframing LMI as a stepping stone to help you get there is a more helpful perspective. Yes, I acknowledge it's a sizeable fee, and you have to pay interest on it, but ask yourself this: in seven years' time, would you regret paying this fee when your home is now worth over $1 million?

To put Australia's capital growth into perspective, dwelling values in Australia increased 382 per cent in the 30 years before July 2022, or 5.4 per cent per annum on average. At that rate, in 30 years' time that $800,000 property would be worth $3 million!

How is LMI calculated?

LMI is calculated based on your loan-to-value ratio (LVR). Since LMI is an insurance product, the riskier the LVR is, the more expensive the premium.

The fees are set by LMI providers and vary from provider to provider, which is why it's imperative to engage a mortgage broker to compare LMI fees. We have two major providers in Australia: Helia (formerly Genworth) and QBE Insurance. Between them, these two providers insure more than 60 per cent of home loans in the country. Westpac, St.George Bank and ANZ provide LMI in-house.

It pays to compare LMI providers. I've worked out the premiums for you on an $800,000 purchase price (see table 5.2, overleaf); you can see the differences in LMI fees at different deposit options.

You are unable to choose your LMI provider directly as each lender has exclusive agreements with one or two providers. However, your mortgage broker can share LMI estimates for each lender with you, and you can then use this information to help you choose your lender and, in turn, your LMI provider.

Table 5.2: LMI fees at different deposit options and with different lenders

	5% deposit ($40,000)	10% deposit ($80,000)	12% deposit ($96,000)	15% deposit ($120,000)
Lender 1	$28,576	$16,488	$11,334	$8296
Lender 2	$29,460	$16,907	$10,890	$8237
Lender 3	$30,324	$15,552	$10,319	$7775
Lender 4	$30,400	$17,352	$11,123	$8024
Lender 5	$30,628	$17,352	$11,123	$8024
Lender 6	$30,877	$17,108	$11,021	$8301
Lender 7	$31,018	$15,364	$10,430	$8427
Lender 8	$31,231	$17,309	$11,152	$8427
Lender 9	$32,647	$18,115	$11,677	$8808
Lender 10	$32,680	$15,984	$11,264	$7956
Lender 11	$32,930	$16,303	$11,021	$8934
Lender 12	$33,285	$16,504	$11,152	$8998
Lender 13	$33,639	$16,639	$11,283	$9124
Lender 14	$33,709	$18,651	$12,005	$9061
Lender 15	$29,814	$16,504	$10,627	$8047
Lender 16	$29,460	$17,980	$11,611	$8744
Lender 17	–	$16,303	$10,496	$7920
Lender 18	–	$21,600	$9152	$6800
Lender 19	–	–	$16,192	No LMI at 85%

Using LMI to your advantage

Circling back to Scott Pape's assertion that LMI is a waste of money (sorry, I promise I'm not trying to pick on him!), there are two ways that LMI can help you in the future:

1. You can get your LMI refunded.
2. You can draw equity from your property and pay less LMI.

There are also 'sweet spots' where the LMI fee drops based on your deposit. This can allow you to purchase a much better property than you would be able to with a 20 per cent deposit while only paying a little LMI. A 12 to 15 per cent deposit can often be a sweet spot, in my experience.

You can get your LMI refunded

It's not widely advertised and there are a few applicable terms and conditions, but it is possible to get an LMI refund. To be eligible, you need to meet the following criteria:

*   The loans that have been covered under the LMI policy are repaid in full and any associated mortgage is discharged within 12 months of the settlement date (in which case a refund of 40 per cent of the premium will apply) or from 12 months to less than or equal to 24 months (in which case a refund of 20 per cent) of the premium will apply.
*   The loans that have been covered have not been in arrears throughout the loan term.
*   The calculated refund is greater than the minimum threshold (any stamp duty is not refundable).

It's something to keep in mind if the value of your home increases and you can refinance to another lender within 24 months. Just bear in mind that while your LMI is refundable based on the conditions outlined here, your LMI premium is not transferable between banks.

You can draw equity from your property and pay less LMI

If you have paid a 10 per cent deposit on your home, your LVR is 90 per cent. Given you have already paid LMI, this means you have the option in the future of drawing equity from your home up to a 90 per cent LVR. This could come in handy if you want to do renovations or purchase an investment property.

To do this, you will need to stay with your original lender (so be aware of this before you refinance away with a different lender) and get your property revalued. The LMI provider will also need to approve this and can then work out how much additional LMI you need to pay on the difference in value.

This is rarely discussed and is a very underrated benefit of paying LMI. While it's not the primary reason to pay LMI originally, it has some longer-term benefits.

If LMI protects the lender, how do you protect yourself?

A common objection to paying LMI is that it benefits the lender and doesn't protect you, the borrower. So, how do you protect yourself? This is part of a broader discussion around protecting your greatest asset – you. Your ability to earn an income and make your repayments hinges on your employment and your health.

If you engage a financial planner, they can provide you with a comprehensive overview of your personal insurance policies. There is a common misconception that coverage within your superannuation will protect you, but LMI means taking on new debt levels, which means you will need to update your protection.

Mortgage protection insurance (MPI) is an option to consider. It can cover you if you're unable to make your mortgage repayments due to unemployment, disability or death. Remember, LMI protects the bank and MPI protects you.

What if you don't want to pay LMI?

There are a few alternatives to consider if you don't want to pay LMI:

- You can save for a 20 per cent deposit.
- Some lenders will accept a 15 per cent deposit without LMI payable.
- You could have the option of considering a guarantor loan. I discuss this in more detail in the next chapter.

Key points

1. Lenders mortgage insurance (LMI) can be seen as a hindrance or a helping hand to get you into the property market, depending on your ability to save for a 20 per cent deposit.

2. Every lender's LMI fee will vary, so it pays to compare and look beyond the lowest interest rate.

3. Paying LMI comes with some future benefits, such as the premium potentially being refundable or reusable, depending on your property plans.

Chapter 6

Guarantor loans, explained

Buying a home with zero deposit is possible using a guarantor loan. This chapter goes into detail about what guarantor loans are, how they work, what options there are and the misconceptions and questions around them.

The Bank of Mum and Dad

Did you know that the ninth-biggest lender in Australia is the Bank of Mum and Dad? Yes, you read correctly; after the four major banks, the next biggest lender of home loans is parents. The Bank of Mum and Dad injected more $2.7 billion into the property market in 2023, and Martin North, a well-known property market commentator and Principal of Digital Finance Analytics (DFA), estimates the total loan portfolio of the Bank of Mum and Dad to be worth $35 billion. This is a staggering number when you think about it. Research from Finder indicates that more than 60 per cent of first home buyers will get some financial support from their parents, which is reflected in figure 6.1.

About 40 per cent of Australians aged 25 to 34 *expect* to call on their parents' help to purchase a property, according to a recent report by the Australian Housing and Urban Research Institute. I've highlighted the word 'expect' as it's moving from a privilege to almost a right for children to receive help from their parents. This speaks volumes about the state of the property market in Australia and how so many Australians need a helping hand from their parents to get their foot in the door. I love the saying 'comparison is the thief of joy' – so many first home buyers and subsequent home buyers compare their financial position to friends or colleagues and wonder how they were able to buy more expensive properties. The Bank of Mum and Dad is often the reason, and while some people may never admit it, with a loan portfolio value of $35 billion it is more commonly called upon than you may have thought.

Figure 6.1: average amount gifted by Aussie parents to help their kids with a house deposit

Source: Finder.

If you are considering asking your parents for help, this chapter outlines your options and the legalities of a guarantor loan, which could sidestep your need to go to the Bank of Mum and Dad.

What is a guarantor loan?

A guarantor loan involves a guarantor offering a property they own to be used as 'security' for you to purchase your own home. The security is in place of you needing or having a 20 per cent deposit; as I explained in the previous chapter, when you don't have a 20 per cent deposit, you either pay LMI or you can use the equity in a guarantor's property to cover the deposit required without needing to save.

Most lenders require a guarantor to be an immediate family member, such as parents, grandparents, siblings or aunts and uncles. Some lenders are a little more flexible and accept extended family members or ex-partners.

This is not an option for every Australian home buyer as some parents (or other family members) don't own their home or simply don't feel comfortable acting as a guarantor. Given this chapter focuses heavily on family and finances, it's really important to understand the facts of what a guarantor loan is and isn't before jumping to conclusions or making assumptions.

Let's look at an example of how a guarantor loan might be structured. Imagine you are purchasing a property for $800,000 and you currently have $50,000 saved up. You are $110,000 short of the $160,000 required for a 20 per cent deposit. However, your parents are open to exploring becoming a guarantor for your loan and they own their home, which has enough equity available for them to draw the required $110,000. This means you would be borrowing a total of $750,000 – the $110,000 guarantor loan plus the $640,000 (80 per cent) home loan – and would be making repayments on this full amount. The goal for you then would be to make repayments on the $110,000 guarantor loan and have the value of your property increase enough to 'release' the guarantor loan from your parents' property as quickly as possible. (I explain this in more detail later in this chapter.)

It's vital to understand no 'cash' is provided in this scenario – the equity in your parents' home is used instead. As it's not tangible like money in a bank account, this is where I often start to see some confusion and misinterpretation creep in.

Figure 6.2 provides an illustration of this example in case you're a visual learner like myself.

Figure 6.2: an example breakdown of an $800,000 property purchase using a guarantor loan

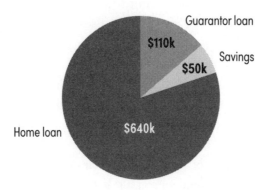

The lender that your parents' loan is currently with is the 'first mortgage', and their bank would need to provide consent for your guarantor loan to be applied against this property, which is known as a 'second mortgage'. It's important to note that not every lender will provide approval for a second mortgage to another bank, so this does come up as an issue from time to time. Parents can then start to get cold feet if they think they need to move their home loan to another lender, which means providing all their documents and information. This is certainly not the case; the goal here is to look for a lender who is able to be a second mortgagor for this loan.

It's at this stage of the guarantor loan discussion that I often start to see the wheels fall off, partly because of the fear of the unknown people have around being a guarantor and the risks attached to it. We discuss the risks in more detail later in this chapter.

If your parents own their home or investment property without a mortgage – banks call this 'unencumbered' – then you would need to find out who holds the physical title deed. This is usually your family's solicitor, though it does surprise me that parents sometimes don't know who holds their physical title deeds. The reason this is important is because when the time comes to settle on your purchase, the bank your loan is approved through will need the title deed to take this property as security. They will then return the title deed once your guarantor loan has been released.

The number of lenders that offer guarantor loans dropped after the Royal Commission into Misconduct in the Banking, Superannuation and Financial Services Industry in 2019, given there were some terrible stories that were exposed. I personally think it's a good move for some lenders to not offer this product as it means the remaining lenders who have chosen to continue offering this type of loan have put a lot of rigour behind their policies. This provides comfort and peace of mind for you (the borrower), your parents (the guarantor), your mortgage broker and the lender. More scrutiny and tighter policies provide the sleep-at-night factor, because an approval ensures all parties are aware of their rights and risks.

What if your parents' home is already being used as security?

It's quite normal and common for parents to have an existing loan against a property they own. In no way is this a deal-breaker for getting a guarantor loan. However, there will need to be sufficient equity available in their property to structure a guarantor loan. To determine this, you will need to work out the LVR of your parents' current loan.

For example, if their property is worth $1.5 million and their current loan balance is $500,000, their LVR would be 33 per cent. If they then provided you with a guarantor loan of $110,000, that would bring their total loan balance to $610,000, increasing their LVR to 41 per cent.

If providing guarantor loan means that your parents' LVR exceeds 70 or 80 per cent, this is potentially an issue. Your parents might have to refinance to another lender, though this is usually a last resort.

How do you release your guarantor loan?

If you're eager to release your guarantor loan and very kindly say 'thank you and goodbye' to your parents' involvement in your home loan, then keep reading. Based on your LVR from when you originally purchased, you will be able to release the guarantor when your property has gone up in value and your loan balance has come down so that you reach 80 per cent LVR on your total loan. The magic number is 80 per cent because you want to avoid paying LMI.

Using the example from the start of the chapter, the purchase price was $800,000 and the value of your total loan was $750,000, giving you an LVR at purchase of 93.75 per cent. In order to bring your LVR down to 80 per cent and release the guarantor loan, if you made no repayments on your loan, you would need the value of your home to exceed $938,000.

In this example, the capital growth required on your home to release the guarantor loan is 17 per cent. To achieve this, some people undertake a small cosmetic renovation such as painting, redoing flooring or just generally cleaning up the property. Other people have been able to ride the coat-tails of strong recent comparable sales in their area that have increased the value of their home in turn. Another way you could achieve this is to refinance your loan to another lender, especially if they have valued your home much higher than your current lender.

Other ways your parents can help you

What happens if your parents don't want to provide their property as security but still want to help you? This situation arises from time to time. Here are a few reasons from my experience why parents can have an aversion to offering their home or investment property as security:

- They may already have a guarantor loan in place for your sibling.
- They may have a number of children, and they feel that if they did it for one child then they'd need to do it for all of them.
- They have plans to sell and move homes, and they don't want a guarantor loan hanging over their heads when they are making decisions.
- They are in a new relationship or perhaps have multiple stepchildren, which has the potential to become messy, especially when there is a financial disparity between the two families.
- They have had a bad experience, or their friends have.
- They have been influenced by a horror story on *A Current Affair*.

All of these reasons are normal, and we each have our own risk profile, so there are no judgements. If parents do wish to help their children financially to get into the property market but aren't comfortable being guarantors, there are alternatives. In my experience, none of these options are very popular, but they may suit some people.

Parent to child loans

A parent to child loan is a home loan product where parents can loan cash to their child at a nominal interest rate that they set, which makes it unique but also quite a niche product. This would suit a parent who doesn't want to provide a property as security but has cash savings.

This cash would normally be earning interest, so by loaning it to their child they would forgo earning interest on their savings. By setting an interest rate they deem suitable, they are not 'gifting' their child the cash and are able to earn some interest during the loan term.

Term deposits

A term deposit is another option for parents who want to provide cash as a security rather than a property. In this scenario, the parents would deposit their cash contribution into a term deposit account under their names with the bank that is funding the home loan, usually for a term around two years. They then earn interest throughout the fixed term. (If the term expires, the lender can roll the funds over into a new term deposit.) It is important to recognise, though, that the funds in the term deposit cannot be withdrawn until the guarantee is ready to be released.

A point to note is that not every lender offers this option, so please check with your mortgage broker if this is an option you want to consider.

Servicing guarantors

A common misconception with guarantor loans is that parents will be assessed on the amount of the loan they are guaranteeing and will need to provide payslips and all their life history. This is not the case for a standard guarantor loan. However, this may be required when they are acting as a 'servicing' guarantor.

Parents may decide to do this when they would like their incomes to be used to help their child, who perhaps is limited by their current level of income in affording the property they want to buy. This does come with an element of risk for the parents as they are committing to being responsible for the loan repayments. This brings a few more variables into the equation. For example, if the parents are going to part-own this property, they will have to pay some stamp duty, and if the child then wants to buy their parents out they will have to pay out that stamp duty to remove the parents from the title. Capital gains tax could also be involved, and if they are in the retirement stage of life, any government benefits they receive could be affected.

If your parents are giving you cash, you need to read this

If your parents are not offering to act as guarantor on a property for you but rather want to give you cash for your purchase, then this is the most important part of this chapter for you. This is common, and it's extremely important to think through all options and consequences. Cash is often the easiest way for parents to help their kids get into the market, but it often comes with strings attached, and lenders want to know: is it a loan or is it a gift?

It is a loan

Some parents lend their children money for a deposit without putting a formal agreement in place but then ask for regular repayments. When there is no prescribed structure for when and how this cash will be repaid, the friction starts to set in, as you might have anticipated. Then, let's say you go on an overseas holiday or buy a new car, and the parents are suddenly asking about your priorities, and so the guilt sets in.

The benefit of a formal loan agreement put down in writing is that it prevents issues arising. If the cash is intended to be repaid, then you should have an agreement drawn up that outlines:

· the amount of the loan
· the intention and context of the loan

- whether interest payments are required or if it is a 0 per cent loan
- whether regular repayments are required
- when the loan will be repaid
- whether the loan will be registered against the title of the property as a caveat
- who the parties to the loan are – for example, will the child's partner be included too?

By far the most important aspect of this situation, which may simmer below the surface but is a tough subject to broach, is the question of what happens if the relationship between the child and their partner breaks down. Life happens, and it's mature to discuss this without being offensive. (I would strongly suggest that the child should initiate this discussion – the parents are thinking it, but would they be brave enough to ask and risk offending the child or their partner?) In the event of a relationship breakdown, if there is no formal loan agreement, then the now ex-partner is entitled to a share of this cash. It's best to engage a family lawyer or solicitor to help you understand the relevant legal implications and obligations.

Other scenarios that could arise include you going bankrupt or, worst-case scenario, passing away. These are definitely not fun scenarios to consider, and it may feel like they are stealing joy from the process of buying your home, but there's a great saying that I think sums it up perfectly: 'Hope for the best, plan for the worst.'

Another important factor to consider is whether this 'loan' will impact your borrowing capacity. If you have a formal loan agreement in place with structured repayments and an agreed loan term, some lenders will factor this into your loan serviceability, which could reduce your borrowing capacity. It's crucial you discuss this with your mortgage broker to find out whether this loan needs to be captured in your serviceability and included as a liability.

It is a gift

All too often I see parents wanting to sign statutory declarations that they are 'gifting' cash to their child for them to buy their own home because the bank has told them this is what's required. The implications are discussed in the risk section later in this chapter.

A gift is non-refundable, which means it is not repayable, and by signing a statutory declaration the parents confirm this in writing. After this, the parents have no recourse to force their child to give the money back. A statutory declaration also exposes this cash gift to being split if the child's relationship breaks down because their now ex-partner can make a claim on it.

My advice is to slow down and be open about how the money will change hands. Too often I see clients who are caught up in the excitement of buying not being organised with their finances, and when the clock is ticking for them to get their loan approved, shortcut decision-making can have severe financial implications for them in the future.

What are the risks?

This is where the guarantor loan conversation usually starts as parents often think in worst-case scenarios. If you recall, I mentioned that lenders look through the lens of 'risk'; in the same way, if you're tapping the Bank of Mum and Dad on the shoulder, then you need to understand the risks.

Before you buy, you absolutely need to consult a financial planner about increasing your personal protection policies that cover you for the extra debt you take on through a guarantor arrangement. In the event that you experience hardship due to cash flow issues, don't pretend it's not happening – contact your mortgage broker or lender. They can put you into a hardship program where your repayments can be deferred (like they did with loan pauses during

COVID-19). You will continue to accrue interest on your loan balance, so it's a temporary bandaid solution. You could also switch to IO repayments, but this would require a reassessment of your loan application. Another option is to rent out your property and move into a cheaper rental if the cash flow works out favourably.

In the event of a relationship breakdown, please make sure you keep making the loan repayments. If you miss repayments on your loan account, it will be reflected on your credit file, making it extremely hard for you to refinance. If you think you will struggle to make the repayments, speak to your mortgage broker or lender to see if the repayments can be paused or deferred.

The absolute worst-case scenario is that you are unable to make the repayments on your home (due to illness, perhaps, or employment issues) and have to sell the property. This should be your last resort as you will only get what's left over after the real estate agent's commission, legal fees and the paying out of your loans.

If the sale of the property does not recoup enough to cover these costs, that's when an element of risk comes into play for the guarantor (your parents), as they are now liable to cover the shortfall. (In extreme circumstances, if they cannot cover the shortfall, their property may be on the line as well, but that is a very worst-case scenario as there are several mediation steps the lender will work through with them before they reach that point.)

What are the benefits?

Having a helping hand to get you into the property market is a privilege. If your parents (or other family members) are willing to assist you, seize this opportunity with both hands. It may allow you to get out of the rental trap and into your own home. (Hello, being able to hang art on the wall without risking your bond!) A guarantor can also ensure you don't pay LMI and provide you with potentially sharper interest rates, too. When structured properly, and with the right legal advice and financial protection in place, it can be a seamless process. I've worked with numerous clients and their parents on harmonious guarantor loan processes that are completely transparent so everyone knows their obligations.

Key points

1. Be open about the level of support you need from your parents. Your parents, in turn, need to be open about what support they can give.

2. Ensure that an agreement is put in place. It can seem like overkill to engage a solicitor or family lawyer, but it's a very small price to pay in the grand scheme of things to be above board and give peace of mind to everyone involved.

3. Be organised and prepared. Guarantor loans are not offered by every single bank, so engage your broker early as there may be more steps involved than you realise.

Chapter 7

Lending policies you need to know about

Each lender has a clear set of guidelines and policies that they follow when it comes to lending money, commonly known as their lending criteria. This chapter explores the five key rules lenders follow when they evaluate each loan application, and also debunks some myths around lending policies.

The five C's

When a lender is considering lending to you, they operate with a framework that is commonly referred to as the 'five C's'. These five factors all have a role to play in how your loan application is structured and which lender is most suitable for you and your purchase. They are:

1. character
2. capacity
3. capital
4. collateral
5. conditions.

The person responsible for reviewing these factors is called a credit manager or credit assessor. They often will ask a mortgage broker for more information if they need some clarity or confidence in order to approve a loan application.

Character

'Character' means profiling you as a borrower. The standard measurement here is your credit file; this is the first filter a lender will apply to your loan application to determine whether they want to lend to you. Your repayment reputation, the amount of debt you have and your credit score will determine whether you get a green light based on the lender's parameters.

Capacity

'Capacity' refers to your ability to borrow and repay. As we discussed in chapter 3, some lenders have clear policies around this. They also apply an array of metrics that are known to mortgage brokers but are not otherwise common knowledge:

- **Debt-to-income ratio (DTI)** is calculated by adding your total monthly debt payments and dividing that by your gross monthly income. Some lenders have strict DTI requirements.
- **Net surplus ratio (NSR)** determines your current debt expenses, proposed debt expenses and living expenses to establish how many times over your income can cover your expenses.
- **Uncommitted monthly income (UMI)** is similar to the NSR calculation; some lenders use one or the other. Your UMI is your available income after all your monthly expenses, which include your loan repayments that have been deducted from your gross monthly income.

Capital

How much you are contributing towards your deposit is your 'capital'. Lenders measure this in terms of risk, so the lower your deposit is, the greater the risk your loan presents to a lender. Any borrower who has less than a 20 per cent deposit is generally required to pay LMI, which protects the lender. Yes, you read that correctly – you need to pay the bank's mortgage insurance premium for lending to you! This is a one-off fee that is usually added to your loan.

Collateral

Collateral is what 'secures' your loan, which is the property you are purchasing. Lenders have very clear guidelines about the types of properties they will and will not lend for. For example, there are only a couple of banks that will lend for an apartment smaller than 50 square metres. These properties are 'risky' in the sense that they are not highly sought after and only suit a small subsection of property buyers. So, if the bank had to take control of this property in the event that you couldn't repay your loan, they would struggle to sell it, which would not be the case for, say, a three- or four-bedroom suburban home in a good area.

Conditions

'Conditions' relates to the details of your loan, such as the loan amount, loan term (the standard is 30 years), interest rate and loan purpose.

Policy mythbusting

Knowing interest rates is only a very small part of mortgage-broking. Being able to problem-solve is where a savvy mortgage broker really earns their stripes and becomes worth their weight in gold.

Lending policies change quite often. Some lenders seek to differentiate themselves from their competitors by offering what are often referred to as 'niches'. They can often feel like the industry's best-kept secrets, so let's look at some of these niches and bust some myths along the way.

Myth: you can't get a loan if you have just started or are in the probation period of a new role

There are a few lenders who will lend to you while you're in your probation period, which is great news if you have just started a new job. They usually want to see a copy of your employment contract and your first payslip. More lender options will be open to you if you have transitioned within your industry (similar role, similar industry but in a new company) and if your gap between roles is less than 30 days.

Myth: you need to have a 20 per cent deposit to buy your home

You can get into the market with as little as a 5 per cent deposit in some cases. The trade-off is that you will need to pay LMI. This is a one-off fee that is usually added to your loan. LMI fees are adjusted based on your deposit contribution – the higher your deposit, the lower your LMI will be.

Myth: you always need to pay LMI if you don't have a 20 per cent deposit

There are brilliant options out there for certain professionals who are exempt from paying LMI. These options may apply to you if you are:

· an accountant (CA or CPA qualified)
· a legal professional (and have a current practising certificate)
· a medical professional (such as a doctor, dentist, optometrist, pharmacist or veterinarian).

Lenders will waive LMI for people in these professions because they are highly employable and have consistent incomes, so they are seen as low risk.

Myth: you can't get a loan while you're on parental leave

There are plenty of lenders that are willing to lend while you are on parental leave. If you are returning to work within a 90-day period, your employer can provide a return-to-work letter that states your income, role title and the date you will recommence. If you're not within the 90-day window, some lenders may want to see a bank account statement that shows you have enough cash savings to cover your loan repayments for the duration of your parental leave. There isn't one black-and-white policy here, which just reinforces that relying on one lender's policies limits your options.

Myth: a pre-approval guarantees that your loan will be approved when you purchase

If there is one thing I've learned in my time as a mortgage broker, it's that clients hate when the goalposts move during their loan application. Getting pre-approved is certainly a step in the right direction to getting your loan approved, but sometimes things change. For example, you could change jobs part-way through your loan application and the lender you were pre-approved with doesn't lend to applicants in their probation period. Another example is that you might purchase a particular type of property that your pre-approval lender doesn't accept, such as an apartment in a high-rise complex or in a particular postcode.

You can imagine how stress levels must rise when you are ready to commit to a purchase and want to sign the contract of sale but need to reapply to a new lender. Don't let this deter you from purchasing, but it's always worth checking with your mortgage broker about the property you are purchasing before putting pen to paper.

Myth: you can't get a loan when you are employed as a casual or contractor

One of the greatest kicks I get from my job comes when I get a loan approved for a client who has been told they can't get a loan because they are employed as a casual or are contracting. There are a number of lenders who will lend to these types of employees. If you are employed casually, lenders want to see your work history, such as your last six month's worth of income, to then calculate what your annual income would be. Being a casual, your hours may vary, so you can understand a lender wanting to know that you will work enough hours to earn the money to make your repayments if they lend money to you.

If you are a contractor, some lenders will want to see your history of contracting. Being a contractor can mean a few different things. You may be on a 12-month project, and so the lender will ask questions such as whether the contract be renewed or whether you can you pick up another contract quite easily. If you contract through an Australian Business Number (ABN), then you may be viewed as self-employed, which brings up questions such as how long your ABN has been registered, for example.

The good news is that I've seen plenty of loans approved for casual and contracted employees. You just need to be prepared to provide some additional details and work history to give a lender confidence in your future income.

Myth: you can't get a loan if you have a low credit score

In chapter 3, I discussed how your credit score is calculated and classified. It is true that most lenders will not approve your loan application if you have a poor credit score, but the good news is that there are lenders who have a policy of not judging your application on your credit score. There are some grey areas – if a missed payment on a car loan or lease can be explained and given some context, and it's below a certain dollar amount, some lenders may be open to accepting this as an exception to their policy.

If you have serious credit history issues, then it may be more helpful to engage a credit repair agency that can look through your credit report and find ways to clean it up – and, hopefully, improve your creditworthiness in turn. The bottom line is to not sit back and take no for an answer; keep knocking on doors until you find someone willing to roll their sleeves up and look at your situation.

Myth: you don't need to disclose 'buy now pay later' products such as Afterpay

A common source of friction between a broker, lender and client is when an undisclosed buy now pay later (BNPL) product rears its ugly head. Banks view these as loans or liabilities that need to be disclosed. When small things like this are left out, a credit assessor might start sniffing around to see if it has been omitted on purpose or by accident, and this causes more headaches than it's worth.

Close these off and get rid of them. You're trying to get a home loan here; don't let a few purchases through a BNPL product cause issues when you're trying to get your loan approved.

Myth: you can't get a loan if you're a non-resident or temporary resident of Australia

If you're a non-resident or temporary resident of Australia, not every lender will welcome you with open arms, but some will be willing to help you call Australia home. They will start by determining what type of visa you are on and whether or not you are purchasing with an Australian citizen. You will need to provide details of your visa and how long you are entitled to work in Australia. You may also have limitations imposed upon your application, such as a higher deposit or a higher stamp duty fee. Don't let these hurdles deter you.

I quite often see clients who get the ball rolling on their loan options while applying for citizenship, so by the time they become Australian citizens they have the confidence to get a loan to buy their home.

Key points

1. Pay attention to the five C's to learn how your loan application will be assessed. Your broker will address these to ensure your loan is approved with as little friction as possible.

2. Be willing to challenge the status quo if you get told 'no' to your application. Lending policies are not black-and-white, and you may just be the exception to the rule.

3. Mortgage myths are just that – myths. Be willing to consider a lender you may not have heard of if they are open to lending to you.

Chapter 8

What happens during your loan application?

Applying for your home loan can elicit a combination of excitement, stress and nervousness. The goal of this chapter is to give you some insights into the steps you'll take throughout your loan application journey so you can feel more confident about what happens behind the scenes and how a lender assesses your application.

Step 1: initial discussion with a mortgage broker

There are approximately 18,000 mortgage brokers across Australia and, like all industries, you have your great, good and mediocre practitioners. However, I would say the majority of mortgage brokers are extremely client-focused and knowledgeable. You want to do your research on a broker or brokerage you feel comfortable with.

To get the ball rolling, you would have an introductory discussion where you share information about yourself and your aspirations, and ask questions. It is important to manage your expectations; you may not get exact numbers, such as your borrowing capacity, at this stage.

The more prepared you are for this discussion, the better:

- **Know your income.** Your gross annual income is the key number. If you are a casual worker, a contractor or are self-employed, then find the relevant income information (as discussed in the previous chapter) and be prepared to give details about your current employment situation.
- **Know your expenses.** If you have done the research outlined in chapter 3, this should be easy. Some expenses, such as HECS-HELP debt balances, you can find out online. If you have car or personal loans, then it's helpful to share the balance and monthly repayments.
- **Know your savings.** How much do you currently have saved up and what are you targeting each month? If you are selling shares or a car, or if you have money in a government scheme such as the First Home Super Saver Scheme (FHSSS), this balance would be very helpful. Also, if you want to set aside a bit of buffer money for your 'Safety' account, then identify your ideal balance to retain here.
- **Know your options.** Share whether you will be exploring the option of getting support from parents in the way of cash or equity.
- **Know whether you want to tap into any available state or federal grants, such as for first home buyers.** These grants have eligibility criteria you will need to meet, such as limits on purchase price, annual income and how long you need to occupy the property.

Another great way to prepare is to write down all the questions you have. Even better, email these questions to your broker prior to your meeting to allow them to prepare answers for you. Try not to rely on remembering your questions as you will be given plenty of information, and sometimes the overload of information can feel a little overwhelming. Given this is a preliminary discussion, you shouldn't incur a fee for this consultation, but it's always best to confirm this with the mortgage broker you engage.

Step 2: sharing your documents and personal information

To provide you with detailed information about your borrowing capacity, lender and loan options, interest rates and repayments, your broker will ask you to supply some information. This is often referred to as a 'fact find'. Let me assure you for your peace of mind that this is not a loan application and none of this information will be shared with a bank.

Brokers all have different ways of requesting and collecting information, but I would caution you to not email sensitive information such as identification documents, payslips, tax returns or account information. Have you verified that your email account is safe and secure? A user-friendly and much more secure way to upload documents and information is through a portal. Ask your mortgage broker if you are unsure what to do, as data protection and security are of utmost importance in our industry.

As part of this stage, you will receive a credit guide that outlines more information about your mortgage broker, the lenders they consistently use and key information about their credit licence. You will also receive a privacy policy document that details how your personal data is collected, stored, used and shared with third parties, such as lenders.

The data you share will allow your mortgage broker to work out your borrowing capacity. If you are going to pay LMI, then your broker will also run an estimate on the LMI fee. Another critical element at this stage is checking lender policies, and in the previous chapter I discussed some key lender policies that you need to be aware of. One thing I've learned in my years as a mortgage broker is that everyone's situation is unique, so your loan requirements need to factor this in.

Your broker will present you with an outline, commonly called a 'preliminary assessment', which summarises the following points:

1. **Your borrowing capacity.** There may be suggestions around paying out HECS-HELP, personal or car loans to increase your serviceability. Another key liability to consider removing is credit cards, which are notorious for driving down your borrowing capacity.

2. **Possible lender options.** Your broker will recommend which lenders are suitable for you and which policies are relevant to your situation. Perhaps their interest rates are competitive, their turnaround times are quick or their policies fit your needs.

3. **Possible interest rates.** If you have indicated a preference for a variable- or a fixed-rate loan, your broker will outline their current rates. Please be aware that lenders' interest rates are constantly moving, and quite often these changes are not even in line with the RBA's rate changes.

4. **Possible repayments.** Your broker will give you very good guidance about what your monthly repayments will be on your home loan so you can work out the difference between this and how much you are currently able to save. You can also think about getting into the habit of budgeting for these repayments by saving extra, or adjusting your budget to see what else you may need to sacrifice to accommodate these repayments. If you are currently paying rent, then you have already had great practice with making regular and consistent repayments.

The reason I've described some of the above points as 'possible' is that the numbers outlined in your preliminary assessment can (and likely will) change based on your final deposit and the purchase price of the home you buy.

The discussion you will have with your mortgage broker at this stage is about whether you need time to save some more for your deposit and which lender to choose to organise your pre-approval.

Step 3: submitting your loan application

Once you and your mortgage broker have confirmed which lender is the most suitable for your situation, the next step is to organise your loan application and sign application forms. Some lenders have been fantastic at adopting digital signatures, while other lenders will require a 'wet' or physical signature. You may also be required to provide updated documents or information, such as a recent payslip or bank statement; for example, if the payslip you initially provided is more than a fortnight old, the bank will ask for your most recent copy. I encourage you to get used to providing extra information; I promise, your mortgage broker is not trying to be difficult. (Trust me, we want to be the exact opposite.)

Once all your documents and forms have been received by your mortgage broker, your loan application can be submitted. Once your broker hits 'submit', a credit check will automatically be triggered. You may have heard that it's not advisable to have multiple loan applications running concurrently; this is because you don't want to have so many hits on your credit file in a very short period. The analogy I use is that we 'measure twice and cut once' when it comes to choosing a lender to submit your loan application to so we avoid you having an overactive credit file.

Once the lender has received your loan application, you will receive an update from your mortgage broker about their current turnaround times. This refers to the number of business days it will take for your application to move through their workflow queue and be reviewed by a credit assessor. This timeframe may have changed since the indication you were given before your loan was submitted, and there could be a few reasons for this:

- **The lender is running a promotion.** Sometimes lenders will run a campaign such as a low-interest-rate or refinance-rebate incentive, and the resulting influx of applications will cause its turnaround times to increase.
- **The lender is short-staffed.** Resource allocation is vital for a lender to maintain consistent turnaround times, and some lenders are better at this than others.
- **Your loan application may be deemed 'complex'.** If you are self-employed or you operate with trusts, your application may need to be allocated to a specialist team of credit assessors, and typically these types of loans take longer to review.
- **Your loan application requires LMI approval.** Some lenders have the authority to approve loans that need LMI in-house, while other lenders will need to refer your loan application to their mortgage insurer.
- **The lender has a longer assessment process.** Different lenders have different processes. For example, some lenders have a 'pre-assessment' stage where all your documents are reviewed and verified before moving through to a credit assessor. If your application is missing any supporting documents, they will request these from your mortgage broker, who will pass that request on to you.
- **The lender is disorganised.** Sometimes, smaller lenders offer a 'special' low interest rate and are not equipped to handle the influx of loan applications. Experienced mortgage brokers see this time and time again and are most likely 'once bitten, twice shy' with certain lenders that have built this reputation for themselves. A mortgage broker will often stake their

reputation on which lender they recommend to clients, and if you're chasing a low rate and have been advised that the lender is notorious for being disorganised, take heed – it's often not worth the hassle.

When your loan application is submitted, some lenders run an algorithm called a 'credit scorecard'. This algorithm's exact formula is a closely guarded secret, but we do know some of the elements that feed into this calculation:

- **Your credit score.** I mentioned earlier that a check on your credit file will be triggered once your application is submitted and your score is incorporated into the algorithm. The information in your credit file will also be matched with the information in your loan application to ensure that it is true and accurate.
- **Whether you are an existing client with this lender.** If so, you will be registered in their database, which can be beneficial as some lenders will favour existing customers.
- **Stability in your current home address.** Lenders don't like you bouncing around, particularly if you have lived in your current address for less than six months.
- **Stability in your current role.** Changing employers isn't a deal-breaker for all lenders, nor is being in your probation period, but some lenders prefer tenure.
- **Your liabilities.** Too many debts will down-score your application, which is why your broker will usually recommend that you pay out and close as many as you can.
- **Your assets.** When you completed your initial fact find, you will have completed a section on your asset position. This matters. If you have a low deposit, it's critical you build your asset position – this is where I see the majority of issues with loan applications. Always remember to include any savings, shares,

superannuation balances, vehicles, properties, jewellery, crypto, art and anything else of value that you own.

- **Your security.** The home you intend to purchase will also be scored, with weighting placed on the postcode and the type of property.
- **Your loan details.** The size of your loan and the LVR will be factored in.
- **Metrics such as DTI and NSR.** If your loan application has you borrowing to your absolute maximum and you have no leftover cash each month, this could present a risk to your loan application. Some lenders have a very clear minimum NSR and maximum DTI they will approve.
- **The level of detail entered into your online loan application.** This is out of your control and is the responsibility of your mortgage broker. Your loan application is entered into an online platform that submits this information to your selected lender, and if it is missing key information or data then your credit scorecard will be downgraded. I've heard through the grapevine that one of the big four lenders adds a favourable weighting if your employer's fax number is entered! The devil is in the details, and the inclusion of a seemingly small piece of data, such as your monthly living expenses, can have a major impact on your loan application.

In rare circumstances, your application may be 'scorecard declined', which means your credit situation falls outside of the parameters set by the lender's algorithm. This is quite a deflating experience as you cannot overturn a scorecard decline – there is no negotiating this. Quite often, poor credit scores, too many current debts or too low a deposit are the reasons for scorecard declines. Lenders have also been known to adjust their algorithms without warning, so a loan application that's similar to one a lender approved six months ago could now suddenly be scorecard declined, catching the mortgage broker unawares. The good news is that some lenders do not operate with an algorithm or credit scorecard.

Outstanding information required

When your loan application is reviewed by a credit assessor, their primary focus is to ensure the lender is happy to lend to you. In the previous chapter I shared the five C's, which are exactly what the credit assessor will have been trained on.

If the credit assessor is missing key information to make their decision, they will request more information from your mortgage broker, who will either see if they have it on file or ask you to supply it. From my years of experience in this industry, this is where friction can start to set in between the assessor, the broker and the borrower (you). Some assessors are wonderful and pragmatic – they take the time to read through an application, review all documents provided, and then call the broker and talk through any missing information and why they need it so the broker can communicate this clearly to the client. Other assessors have great technical knowledge but perhaps lack empathy for the client experience and will make requests for information that a broker can't understand, and this can be frustrating for the broker and for you.

I try to break down requests for more information into two key categories:

1. **Loan-critical.** This is information that is vital for your serviceability, such as evidence of your last two years of bonus payments or commissions, or confirmation that your credit card or personal loan has been closed out in full. It should be clear why a lender would want to see this information to make their decision, but in some circumstances you might wonder *Why are they asking for so much information when we've*

provided this already? or *Is this jeopardising my loan application?* It's normal to experience these feelings at this stage as a little doubt creeps into your mind as to whether the lender is going to approve your loan. Release this emotion and ask your broker what their interaction with the assessor was like – are they open to discussing your loan, and will they keep asking for more information?

2. **Not loan-critical.** Perhaps you haven't changed your maiden name to your married name, or you just need to provide an outline of your current car lease statement to verify your monthly repayment. These requests can seem minor, but it is still important to a lender that their responsibilities have been met by ensuring they have all the correct data on your file. It is also common for there to be multiple information requests. As much as I try to avoid back and forth between clients and credit assessors, sometimes hurdles appear unexpectedly; I encourage you to take it in your stride and zoom out to see the bigger picture here.

Genuine savings requirements

During your research, you may have read about the need for genuine savings for your deposit. This can lead to a little confusion or misinterpretation. 'Genuine savings' is the requirement to have, typically, a 5 per cent deposit saved up over a three-month period, which demonstrates to the lender your ability to regularly save.

If you are currently renting, then quite a few lenders will accept a copy of your rental ledger – which shows you have paid your rent on time, every time – in lieu of the need to save consistently for three months. You will need to ensure your name is on the lease of the property and your rental repayment conduct is clean.

You can meet the genuine savings requirement by selling shares or your car, or by receiving funds from your family. Depending on the lender and their policies, you may not need to provide evidence of genuine savings if your deposit is over 5 or 10 per cent. There are also a handful of lenders that don't have a genuine savings requirement.

Step 4: pre-approval

A great research report produced by Aussie Home Loans and Lonergan Research called *Property Possibilities: Buyers' Outlook Report* shared a few alarming insights:

- Two thirds of property buyers (66 per cent) have reported missing out on a property because they were not ready (such as because they did not have pre-approval).
- Almost half (49 per cent) don't understand the deposit percentage required to buy a property.
- More than two in five (41 per cent) are confused about the pre-approval process.

I'm hoping your time spent reading this book and educating yourself means that you don't end up contributing to statistics like these. With so much information available, being resourceful and taking the initiative to learn what needs to happen next sets apart the buyers who get pre-approved. Be willing to pick up the phone and ask your broker questions.

It is such a great feeling when the lender issues your pre-approval. (Some lenders may refer to it as 'approved in principle' or 'conditional approval'.) Most pre-approvals are valid for three months, but don't stress about having to find the perfect home during this period; some lenders may allow you to extend for another three months if you provide updated payslips and a consent form. Some lenders may ask for your whole application to be resubmitted, though, so double-check with your broker about the length of time your pre-approval is valid for and the renewal process.

Here are some of the advantages of being pre-approved:

- Real estate agents will ask if you are pre-approved as a filter to see if you are a qualified prospect, which increases your chances of them taking you seriously and improves your conversations with them.
- You have confidence in how much you can borrow and how much you can purchase for.
- Your energy can go into choosing your home, not choosing your home loan.

You may hear of people who were pre-approved but had their pre-approval withdrawn when they went to put pen to paper on their contract of sale. Here are a few reasons why this might have happened:

- Their purchase price exceeded the maximum amount set.
- Their personal situation changed – maybe they changed jobs or had a baby.
- Their financial situation changed – their deposit wasn't high enough, or they took on a new debt, such as a car loan.
- The property wasn't accepted by their lender.
- The lender changed its policies or lending criteria.
- Interest rates increased, which impacted their borrowing capacity.

A written letter confirming your pre-approval is not a guarantee, but it is the next best thing and will enable you to purchase with confidence. It provides the reassurance you need to bid at an auction or make an offer. The best way to reduce your stress at this stage is to talk to your broker *before* making your offer. This is a time-sensitive conversation; share with your broker the property, purchase price and your up-to-date deposit amount to ensure your broker can give you the green light that there is not going to be an issue with your borrowing capacity.

Step 5: finding your property

Once you're pre-approved, it's time to pound the pavement and actively start house hunting. I expand on this in detail in chapters 9 and 10.

Step 6: getting your loan formally approved

To transition from pre-approval to getting your loan unconditionally approved (also known as 'formal approval') your broker will request additional documents, such as:

- a copy of the front page of the contract of sale that is signed by you
- an updated copy of your savings account statement reflecting your current balance
- a recent payslip
- any missing information, such as credit card closure letters.

Your signed contract of sale is vital as that is required for your mortgage broker and lender to order the valuation of your property. If there is a cooling-off period, then the clock is ticking, and everyone needs to be organised as you may have as little as five days to get your loan approved. The ideal workflow is for your broker and solicitor or conveyancer to be in direct contact with one another and ensure you are copied into emails. You don't want to be the messenger at this point, nor should you need to be.

You will also need to pay your holding deposit into the real estate agent's trust account and receive a receipt for this.

Your mortgage broker may mention a few terms that you may be unfamiliar with:

- **Escalation** is when your broker asks for your loan application to be bumped up the queue as a priority given you are in a cooling-off period and an approval is time-critical. Some lenders are great at escalations while some lenders are downright hopeless, irrespective of how many times you call and email them.

- Each lender assigns a **business development manager (BDM) or relationship manager (RM)** to a mortgage broker. They are the broker's key point of contact for raising escalations or troubleshooting any issues during the loan application process.
- Lenders' lending policies can be quite rigid, but some lenders may be open to providing a **policy exception** if they are given the right information, documentation and evidence. Policy exceptions are given on a case-by-case basis and sometimes come down to the strength of the relationship your broker has with the lender or their prior experiences getting policy exceptions.

Valuation

In order for your loan to be formally approved, the lender will arrange a valuation of the property. The valuer determines whether the price you paid for the property is in line with their *opinion* of what the property is worth. I've deliberately used the word 'opinion' because valuations are subjective. Each lender will have a 'panel' of independent valuation firms they will engage to undertake an inspection and provide a thorough valuation report. The valuation report is a detailed analysis of the property and includes:

- council zoning, planning and restrictions
- property and land size
- number of bedrooms
- location
- building structure and condition
- fixtures and fittings
- vehicle access to the property (such as driveways and garage)
- recent sales and similar properties in the area
- areas for improvement

- standard of presentation and fit-out
- other market conditions.

The most important part of the report is the assessed value, which everyone wants to see come back in at the purchase price. A valuation is ordered *after* you purchase your property. There is no way to know if a valuer will agree on your final purchase price until after you have signed a contract of sale, which clearly states your purchase price. The contract of sale is required in order to request a valuation, so there is no chance of gaming the system.

There is an alternative: you could pay for your own independent, pre-purchase valuation to be completed by a certified practising valuer (CPV), which could help with your negotiations. If the property holds a higher emotional value to you, such as being around the corner from a great school or close to your parents, then you may be inclined to pay a premium for this property, which won't be factored into how a valuer assesses the value of the home you buy.

I would say that valuation is the most critical stage in going from pre-approval to formal approval, and it is out of the broker's and lender's control. A valuer has the ability to make or break the loan approval if their valuation report provides information that the lender doesn't like – for example, being too close to powerlines or having an unapproved dwelling such as a granny flat on the property – or their appraisal figure is lower than your purchase price.

Your lender will arrange one of four types of valuation (and will typically choose a more detailed valuation method if there is a higher perceived risk to the lender):

1. A **full valuation** is the most detailed and comprehensive method. The valuer will physically inspect the property inside and out and write up their property valuation report. This report will include photos, property details and the justification behind their assessment. This is the most common

type of valuation when you purchase your home, The lender's appointed valuer will contact the real estate agent to arrange access for their inspection. You will not need to be present for this; some people believe you can influence the valuer, but this is not the case.

2. A **kerbside valuation**, also known as a drive-by valuation, is where the valuer physically inspects the property but only from the outside. This is not as thorough as a full valuation. The property valuation report will factor in recent comparable sales and the external condition of the property, though given they don't go inside, none of the internal features will be factored into the valuation.

3. A **desktop valuation** is undertaken by valuers without any physical inspection of the property. Given this is a digital assessment, the valuer's points of reference for assessing the property's value are the available property details and recent comparable sales data.

4. An **automated valuation** (AVM) is an algorithm-based method using a number of factors to produce a result. It will factor in recent comparable sales, market data and property information to provide a fast valuation result.

You might be wondering, *What happens if the lender's valuation report comes in less than my purchase price?* This has happened only a handful of times during my last seven years in mortgage broking, and the good news is that we've always been able to find a workaround. Often this happens when the property market is going through a transition period, such as recovering from a downturn, and valuers are relying on old sales data. While it sounds like the worst-case scenario, there are some possible solutions:

1. **'Challenge' the valuer's report.** If there is sales data the valuer has missed or overlooked, you can work with your mortgage

broker (and sometimes the real estate agent) to lodge a challenge. This means the valuer has to review the properties that you think are comparable (similar specifications, similar suburb and sold within the last three to six months). It can take up to five business days for the valuer to do their review and provide feedback. Based on my experience, this is a long shot, as valuers are generally quite confident with their initial assessment and don't have too much empathy if their valuation jeopardises your loan approval.

2. **Go to another lender and order another valuation.** As you may recall, different lenders have different valuers on their panel. By ordering a valuation with a different lender, a different valuer may be assigned to your property purchase. This is known as an 'upfront' valuation, as you won't have submitted a loan application but rather ordered a valuation to ensure it returns at your purchase price; if it does, then you can submit your application to be formally approved. The main consideration is to ensure you have lender options to fall back on.

3. **Order a 'check' valuation.** This is a little-known secret in mortgage broking! If you are stuck with a specific lender and their valuation falls short then, depending on the lender, your broker can sometimes request a 'check' valuation, which is where this lender orders a second independent valuation report from a different valuation firm. I've called on this option a few times and achieved favourable outcomes.

4. **Order an independent valuation.** Similar to the pre-purchase valuation, this is completed by an independent valuer that you engage and pay directly. This can be helpful before going to an auction or if there are not enough recent comparable sales, or if the property is unique or has undergone significant renovations and the real estate agent hasn't given a clear price indication.

5. **Proceed with the sale.** Be aware, though, that if you have the option to remain with the loan application your broker submitted with your lower lender valuation, it will change your final LVR and possibly your interest rate. For example, imagine your purchase price is $800,000 and the valuation is $750,000, and your requested loan amount is $560,000 – what was originally a 70 per cent LVR is now going to be 75 per cent. If your LVR goes above 80 per cent, you will incur LMI, which is when you could consider changing banks. Your interest rate changes if your lender changes their rates based on your LVR, so it's also worth double-checking this with your broker.

As you can see, the valuation part of your loan application process can be quite the roller-coaster and, as I've mentioned, is largely out of your control. Be prepared to take guidance from your mortgage broker and ask them about their past experiences with valuation issues.

Final steps

Once the lender has asked for all their additional documents and information and then completed your valuation, your loan can be formally approved. There is no better feeling for a broker than calling the client and saying, 'Your loan has been approved!' Your mortgage broker will send you a copy of the formal approval letter and also email a copy to your solicitor or conveyancer. The formal approval letter will outline your loan amount, interest rate and loan purpose.

Shortly afterwards your loan contract will be sent to you. Depending on the lender, your loan documents may be issued digitally for you to sign, emailed for you to print and sign or posted to you. Your mortgage broker will then usually arrange a time to walk you through your loan documents and make sure all the details are correct and match up to the formal approval information.

Once your loan documents have been signed, if they are paper-based then I highly recommend scanning copies to keep on file and posting them back to the lender via registered post. Lenders have lost forms on occasion, or they go missing in the mail, and you just don't want to leave this to chance, especially when you have your settlement date scheduled. The small act of scanning documents to keep on file could mean avoiding issues down the track.

Once your loan has been formally approved, you will also pay the remaining balance of your deposit, which is usually transferred to your solicitor's or conveyancer's trust account. At this stage, you will exchange your signed contract of sale with the vendor's signed contract of sale, which seals the deal – you have officially purchased your home! Congratulations!

Most lenders will ask you to arrange your building insurance (also known as a 'certificate of currency') when you exchange contracts. This means you will need to call your insurance provider and provide details of the property you have purchased, such as the value of the home, when it was built and, most importantly, who the 'interested party' is, which is the lender who has approved your loan. You will need to provide a copy of your certificate of currency to get to settlement, so get this organised nice and early.

If you are renting then you also want to consider the right time to give notice to vacate. You need to refer to your rental agreement to find out if you can give four weeks' notice without penalty or if you need to see out the fixed term of your lease, then speak with your property manager to discuss your obligations and any costs you will incur. You also need to factor in moving out and doing your end-of-lease clean. I strongly recommend that you do *not* make your settlement date and your end-of-lease date the same day. Just think of the stress you will incur when you have a moving truck booked and sitting in the driveway while you're sweating on confirmation that your settlement has taken place! Give yourself a few extra days to move out of your rental property. This will allow you to move into your new home with less stress and give you time to arrange a thorough end-of-lease clean. It will also provide breathing room if there is a delay with the settlement, which could come from an issue on the vendor's side and therefore be out of your control.

Purchasing your own home ranks right up there among life's most pivotal achievements. The next part of this book goes into detail about your property search and guides you through the property hunting and negotiating process.

Key points

1. Be as organised as possible, as the loan application and approval process can be like a game of snakes and ladders sometimes.

2. Ask your broker if you have backup options for lenders in the event of delays, policy changes or issues with your valuation.

3. Use the time available to your advantage and don't leave actioning requests to the last minute. It's already a stressful experience, so try to avoid extra stress by ensuring your team are in communication with one another too.

PART II
BUYING YOUR HOME

Chapter 9

Property types

One of life's big decisions is where you buy your home and what home to buy. This decision will have a major impact on your lifestyle and your social network. It's a decision that can't be made just by looking on realestate.com.au or Domain – it's going to take pounding the pavement, speaking to plenty of real estate agents and investing energy into making a confident decision.

The research isn't pretty: the average buyer will look at more than 300 property listings and attend more than 11 open homes before they get serious enough to make an offer, according to realestate. com.au. Buying a home is a big decision. *The 2020 St.George Home Buying Survey* found that it takes first home buyers an average of 44 hours to research properties, do the due diligence on one they like and then begin the home-buying process, which includes applying for a mortgage. When you put it into perspective, that's only one week of your life – though it might feel much longer than that given the whole process is spaced out over time. If you can reframe it that achieving your dream of buying a home is a privilege, not a right, then it only makes sense to take your time, try to enjoy the process and recognise that it will be a distant memory one day.

Let's take a step back first and look at the different types of property available to you.

Off the plan

An 'off-the-plan' purchase is where you purchase an apartment or unit before construction has even commenced. You may base your purchase off a 3D model, a set of blueprints or a shiny brochure about a building complex or project that a developer is planning to commence. In order for the developer to even get finance to begin their project, most lenders require them to pre-sell at least 80 per cent of the development.

There is a lot of polarising commentary around off-the-plan purchases – some advocate for them while others detest them. So, how do you decide if an off-the-plan purchase will suit your needs? Here are some things to consider:

- **First home buyer discounts.** Depending on the purchase price and your state or territory's concessions for first home buyers, you may be eligible for waived stamp duty or a grant when you purchase a brand new property under a price threshold.
- **Timing.** Determine the expected date of completion and then allow for delays, which are quite normal. A longer timeframe could work in your favour as it means more time to save for your deposit. However, delays could also present an issue if your personal or financial situation changes before settlement because you are committed to going through with the purchase.
- **Capital growth or negative equity.** Because you buy the property today before it is built, the property market could surge while construction is underway, and by the time your property is due for completion it may have increased in value. However, you also need to consider the opposite: the broader property market could fall, or if your property is part of a large development project then there is a risk that lenders may not value your property for what you purchased it for.

- **Builder risk.** If your builder has cash flow or compliance issues, that can jeopardise your property being completed. When you are researching a project, it is highly recommended that you look at the previous projects completed by the developer, builder and architect. Try to determine the quality of their completed projects and, if possible, find out if there were any delays with completion and settlement.
- **Choice of fixtures and finishes.** You may have a few options to choose from, allowing you to personalise your property. However, there may be additional costs associated with this.
- **Deposits and costs.** You will need to check the deposit requirements with your conveyancer or solicitor. A 5 per cent deposit may be required, or the minimum could be 10 per cent. You also need to be aware of your stamp duty requirements, if applicable, and this could be due 12 months from your purchase date.
- **Builder's guarantee.** You will be protected with a builder's guarantee. Each state and territory has slightly different levels of protection for what is covered and for how long. It is definitely worth looking into this to see what type of guarantee is available for your build and how it could protect you.
- **Strata or body corporate fees.** With an apartment or unit, there will be a regular expense (usually quarterly) to contribute to the ongoing maintenance of the common areas. Facilities such as lifts, gyms, pools, gardens, parking and roofing are some of the items covered. It's worth getting a feel for strata or body corporate fees so you can factor them into your future cash flow as you don't want them creeping up on you unexpectedly.
- **Interest-rate changes.** Similar to the price fluctuation risk, you also need to consider the implications of interest rates going up during the build period. This may affect your borrowing capacity and, therefore, your ability to settle. Just bear in

mind that while you can be pre-approved before the build commences, you won't be given formal approval until the property is completed and settlement is called.

- **Settlement timings.** A significant challenge from a finance perspective is that settlement can be called with two weeks' notice, which doesn't give you very much time to get formal approval in place and get ready to settle. Stay in contact with your solicitor and developer for regular updates, and try to start your loan application at least a month out from your expected settlement date to give you enough time to settle without the stress.

House and land

A house and land 'package' is when you purchase a block of land and the construction of a home on the land. It's one purchase that comes with two contracts – one for the land component and one for the build component. One of the biggest advantages of purchasing a house and land package is that stamp duty is paid on the purchase price of the land, not on the total value of the land and build. Also, you may be eligible for first home buyer grants or discounts, such as not paying stamp duty if your land purchase or total build falls under a given limit.

The reason it's referred to as a 'package' is that the land and construction contracts may go through the same developer. Packages generally come with different tiers of inclusions:

- **Standard inclusions** can include a fully completed kitchen, bathrooms, doors and windows, electricals, flooring and built-in wardrobes.
- **Additional inclusions** can include landscaping, fencing and driveways.

- **Premium inclusions** can include wooden floorboards, integrated and upgraded appliances, and stone or marble benchtops.

If you are purchasing through a developer, they will have a shortlist of builders and home designs to fit the area. You may have some options to choose from, which is something to ask about in the lead-up to purchasing. From a finance perspective, it is highly recommended to speak with your mortgage broker about your maximum borrowing capacity to make sure you have a gauge on how much you can spend on upgrades and finishes. The reason this is so important is because when you head into the studio with the builder to make your selections, you will be deciding on everything from colours to flooring styles, any changes to the layout, and even little details such as handles and floor drains! To the unprepared, this process can lead to decision overload and be quite daunting. Take a step back before you get to this stage and decide your non-negotiables and what your budget allows for so you can avoid the builder coming back to you with a quote that blows you out of the water.

Use your time wisely by going to as many display homes as possible and getting a feel for what you love, like and loathe. Just a word of warning, though: the homes in the display village are usually of the highest specifications with all the bells and whistles! The builders go all out to showcase what they are capable of, and it will certainly whet your appetite. Energy ratings, environmental sustainability and solar are also of high importance, so make sure you give these things some consideration too.

To get finance approval for your house and land package, you will get your land loan and settle on your land first. You will then need to provide your lender with your building contract, council-approved plans and any items not included in your contract (for example, your landscaping), and they will then arrange a valuation. This will be completed by one of the lender's valuers, who will assess your land value and the total cost of your build to provide their professional assessment of the end value of your home. In the event that your valuation comes in lower than your total purchase price, you can follow the process I outlined in chapter 8. Once the valuation is complete, you can get your construction loan, and you will make progress payments directly to your builder. As your build nears completion, you will finalise the 'certificate of occupancy' (OC); this is the last piece of the puzzle to complete your property purchase and finalise your loan.

At this stage, you will have two loan accounts: your land loan and your construction loan. A common request is to merge these two loans, which sounds reasonable, but it isn't straightforward. The reason is that the two loans have different start dates, which affects the way the repayments are calculated over a 30-year loan term, something banks call 'amortisation'. A possible solution is to refinance your loans 'internally', which means staying with your current lender and providing them with your payslips and updated personal financial details; they will usually complete a desktop valuation and then, once approved, you will sign your new loan documents and your loans will be merged in your internet banking. An alternative option is to refinance your loans with another lender. An advantage of doing this is that your property will undergo a full valuation, which comes with two possible benefits: your LVR may be lower, which gives you access to lower interest rates, and your property's value may have increased, so there may be equity you could access for either an investment property or shares.

Existing property

Buying an existing property is the favoured approach for many home buyers as they can see the property and move in as soon as possible.

In this section, I break down the different types of properties you can purchase and what you need to be aware of when buying.

Unit or apartment

If you are younger, then a unit or apartment is usually a good place to start your property journey from an affordability and location perspective. There is plenty of debate about whether buying an apartment is a good idea, which is not helpful, especially if you want to buy in a capital city and have a limited deposit and borrowing capacity. My suggestion is to look at your budget and buy what you can afford when you can afford to.

A great location can greatly impact an apartment's value; this means choosing an apartment in a quality suburb and ideally on a great street. Views are priceless, but you have to hope they won't be interrupted by future developments. A north-facing aspect will push the value of your apartment higher as this can be important for liveability. Study nooks are also becoming quite popular, as is adequate storage. In addition, great amenities and convenient transport options at the doorstep make an apartment desirable for future investment purposes.

A unit or apartment can be a great entry point to the property market, especially if you intend to access government support through a first home buyer grant. One important condition is that you generally need to live in the property for at least 12 months. A way to turn this into an advantage for you is to find an apartment in a good location that may need some cosmetic renovations such as painting, redoing the flooring or perhaps updating the kitchen or bathroom, which has the potential to provide the greatest value uplift. Doing renovations on your new home can be exciting, but be careful not to overspend, especially if you intend to turn this property into an investment once you move out. 'Overcapitalisation' is when the money you spend on renovating doesn't give you a positive return on your investment. Taking the time to plan, budget and think about the functionality of your apartment can avoid costly errors.

My first purchase was a unit in North Parramatta, 24 kilometres north-west of Sydney, and I had no idea what I was doing. I purchased the property for $345,000 and was able to receive $7000 through a first home buyer grant. Little research went into this purchase; if I had done my due diligence, I would have seen the cemetery across the road. It was located at a busy intersection and there was no public transportation nearby. It also got very little sunlight, which I learned the hard way while living there as none of my clothes would dry! On the upside, it was a two-bedroom unit with car parking, which helped with getting more for rent and made it appealing to buyers when I decided to sell it.

Bernadette and I learned an expensive lesson about over-capitalising with this property. Before we sold it, we undertook a complete renovation – bathroom, kitchen, flooring, paint, roof and cupboards. We had a budget, which we did stick to, and we were proud of the finished product. It became clear when we listed the property, though, that we had out-renovated the market. Buyers didn't see the value in what we had done, and our work didn't improve the saleability of our property. In hindsight, we could have achieved the same result with just a few cosmetic improvements, such as fresh carpet and a lick of paint, and perhaps some love to the kitchen and bathroom. We did learn a lot from the process – it was a huge lesson to 'start with the end in mind'. We debriefed afterwards about what result we wanted and what we could or should have done differently to achieve this.

Undoubtedly one of the most overlooked and underrated aspects of purchasing an apartment is the strata report, which provides a summary of the current financial position of the building and any potential future issues you need to be aware of. When you purchase an apartment or unit, you are buying into the whole complex, and amenities such as the lifts, gardens, car parking, gym and pool require maintenance and upkeep, which is the responsibility of the strata. Other considerations include the age of the building, what works have already been completed and what works will need to be undertaken in the future. For example, since the 2017 Grenfell Tower tragedy in West London, there has been a focus on cladding standards for apartment buildings; the cost of replacing cladding would fall under 'capital works' and would not have been factored into the strata's budget, so this is one example of when a 'special levy' could arise and hit you with bill shock. Strata reports can be hundreds or sometimes even thousands of pages long, so you'll need the help of a legal professional with a trained eye who knows what to look for and can determine whether the property is a deal-breaker or deal-maker. Some examples of issues that can come up include the capital works forecast, confusion over by-laws, building defects and builders' warranty insurance, and whether the building's insurance is up to date and the building is over- or under-insured.

Townhouse or villa

A villa is usually a single-level dwelling, whereas a townhouse is two storeys. They can provide a great entry point into the property market, allowing you to purchase in a better location than you might be able to afford if you were purchasing a freestanding house. They are a happy medium between apartments and freestanding houses: they are generally more spacious than apartments but require less maintenance than freestanding houses. However, poor noise insulation could make you feel like you're living in an apartment. When you're looking for a townhouse or villa, it's important to determine how many common walls the property has.

Here are some other points you will need to give some consideration to:

- Would you consider turning it into an investment property, or would you prefer to sell it?
- How much value could you add to the property while you live there?
- If you are planning to start a family or have children, is the home child friendly? How long do you think you could live in the property before you outgrow it, given you will be limited in the structural renovations you could undertake?

Another major consideration when buying a townhouse or villa is the body corporate fees, which are similar to the strata fees when buying an apartment. This is the regular contribution you make to the maintenance of all the properties on the block, including driveways, guttering, lawn and garden maintenance, and fencing.

Duplex or semi-detached property

Very similar to a townhouse, a duplex or semi-detached home gives you more space than an apartment and is ideal if you can't quite afford to purchase a freestanding home in the area. A key difference between these types of properties over townhouses and villas is that you get more land and you only share one common wall with a neighbour. Semi-detached houses are more common in inner-city suburbs, whereas duplexes are more common in the outer suburbs, where larger blocks of land have been subdivided to make way for a more modern style of living.

The considerations when buying a duplex or semi-detached home are similar to those for townhouses and villas. Given you have less ability to make structural changes to the property, you really need to weigh up your liveability in the property over the long term.

Freestanding house

The allure of having your own freestanding house can undoubtedly be traced back to the traditional Great Australian Dream of a home on a quarter-acre block. While the times have changed and there is less need for such a large land size, I can absolutely understand the allure of the freedom that this property type offers – privacy, no need for strata and the ability to make changes as you wish.

Being in a position to buy your own freestanding home is exciting and comes with endless opportunities, such as being able to do your own renovations, extensions or even go all in with a knock-down rebuild. Any purchase of this scale can be daunting for the uninitiated, though, so my general feedback is to 'slow down to speed up'. Use your time wisely to plan, do your due diligence and have hard discussions about what you want to buy and where. There is nothing more unfortunate than clients who have purchased their own home only to then realise that the plans they had in mind would not be approved by the council, or that the home they bought is full of overlooked defects that need repairs.

Here are some of the considerations you want to factor in when buying a freestanding house:

· **What can't be changed.** You can't change the suburb or street once you have bought, so make sure you have done your research before you put pen to paper. Do your homework about the areas you can afford to buy in and how they stack up from an accessibility, community and commute perspective. Buying on a busy street means noise, traffic and parking issues, and don't expect these to change. Budget constraints are naturally a factor, but when possible it's recommended to buy a house in a great position in a good suburb rather than a poor position in a great suburb.

- **The aspect of the property.** North-facing properties tend to attract a premium in Australia. Real estate veteran John McGrath has commented that north-facing properties will often outperform south-facing properties in value by 20 to 25 per cent. For a house, you want a north aspect at the rear so your backyard and the main living areas of your home get plenty of natural light.

- **The block.** Often overlooked, I would say the block is a critical factor when it comes to liveability and lifestyle. A sloping block presents all sorts of issues, such as flooding when it rains, and restricts what you can do in terms of extensions, which can cost significantly more. A flat block undoubtedly comes at a premium, but your future self will thank you for choosing it.

- **Planned infrastructure and developments.** Speaking with real estate agents and looking through local or state plans for development in the area will give you an indication if this will help your property appreciate in value or hinder its capital growth. If there are plans for new roads, tunnels or transport investment, it could mean a few years of pain during the construction phase, but once completed it could be extremely beneficial.

Properties lenders don't like

The kinds of properties lenders don't like are generally also the types of properties that don't perform as well as others, so use this as a guide for properties to avoid. You will often find that these properties are 'reasonably priced' online, but this is for a very good reason: there are fewer lenders willing to finance them or certain restrictions have been placed on these properties.

Here are some of the types of properties lenders generally don't like:

- studio apartments with less than 50 square metres of floor space
- properties within 100 metres of high-tension power lines
- properties right next to train stations
- 'high-density' apartments
- company-titled properties
- properties that are in flood or bushfire zones
- properties with over ten hectares of land
- rural properties that are not connected to utilities.

Key points

1. Have a think about what types of property are both affordable and suitable for your lifestyle now and in the future. If you think you will outgrow a property within two years, then you may need to rethink it.

2. Do your due diligence on the actual property you want to purchase, and on what can and cannot be changed. This will give you an indication of what work you need to do to enjoy the property and how much this work will cost you.

3. Always ensure the property you are buying is acceptable to your chosen lender. Some properties raise red flags for lenders, and this may be for reasons you wouldn't think of. Ask your broker before you sign the contract of sale.

Chapter 10

The home-buying experience

Allianz Insurance published a great piece of research that found, 'Given the stress of buying a home 55 per cent of Aussies say they would rather stay in their current home longer', and, 'searching for a new home affects the mental and emotional wellbeing of more than half (51 per cent) of Aussie home buyers'. These are such unfortunate statistics; buying a home should be a joyous milestone that ought to be celebrated, but somehow it's turned into an unenjoyable and stressful experience. This is backed up by similar feedback from a survey conducted by Moneybox Homebuying (and reported by Mortgage Introducer), in which 37 per cent of those interviewed said that 'buying a home was one of the most stressful life events they had experienced – worse than looking for a job (28 per cent), planning a wedding (23 per cent), and having a child (18 per cent)'.

It's no wonder that the home-buying experience is wrought with stress and anxiety. Who do you trust? What happens next? What costs should you expect? When should the next step take place? Who is responsible for what and when will they get back to you? Let's peel back the layers.

My ten-point property plan

Too often I see home buyers get the order wrong when it comes to buying their home. They follow a process like this:

1. Search for properties online.
2. Go to property inspections.
3. Fall in love with a property.
4. Apply for a loan.
5. Get a conveyancer to review the contract of sale.
6. Make an offer.
7. Do a building and pest inspection.
8. Try to negotiate and make an offer without a cooling-off period.
9. Stress out wondering whether the lender will approve the loan.
10. If the lender approves the loan, sign loan documents and more forms; otherwise, go back to square one.

It's no wonder so many Australians find the home-buying experience stressful. So, let's break down the ideal home-buying journey to minimise your stress levels and increase your confidence to make an offer and buy successfully.

1. Research areas

Once you have determined your budget, look at the suburb you want to live in, then expand your search to a couple of surrounding neighbourhoods. This will give you a feel for how properties in your desired area compare to similar properties in a suburb perhaps ten minutes away. The best thing to do is jump onto Google Maps and print out maps of each suburb you are considering purchasing in, then grab a few coloured highlighters to identify your ideal buying zones, the sections you will consider and the parts that are firm noes (such as busy streets and streets right next to schools, perhaps).

2. Determine what you are looking for

Make your list of 'wants', 'nice to haves' and 'firm noes'. For example, you may be absolutely certain you do not want to live on a busy road or adjacent to a school, shopping centre or hospital. You may want to live in a three-bedroom house but could consider a two-bedroom property that can be extended or renovated.

3. Consider what can or cannot be changed

Please don't allow yourself to get hung up on the colour of the flooring or paint – these can be changed. The slope of the block, backing onto a busy road or being flood-prone zoned is very hard to change, if not impossible. You need to look at the non-negotiables of each property to see what can be changed to suit your lifestyle and requirements, then compare this to a property that ticks all your boxes, and then work out the difference in the purchase price. This will give you an understanding of what compromises you may need to make if you can't afford your dream home.

4. Inspect as many properties as you can

Did you know that the average buyer will look at more than 300 property listings on average and spend nine months searching before they find 'the one'? The more properties you look at, the better you will train your eye to see potential issues, such as a lack of sunlight in the property. You may also realise that the photos on the property listing online don't show a massive tree at the front of the property, or the rooms are actually much smaller than you expected. Take the experience in your stride and recognise that going to multiple property inspections is part of the home-buying journey.

5. Go to multiple auctions

It would shock you how common it is that the first auction hopeful home buyers attend is for the property they are planning to buy.

Each auctioneer has their own style, and each auction has its own rhythm. Attending as many auctions as possible will give you a feel for how they unfold and the different strategies that are at play. YouTube is also a great resource for researching recent auctions held by the auctioneer or the real estate agency that you may purchase through.

6. Spend some time in the area

If you're buying in an area that you are unfamiliar with, then think about spending a few weekends there to get familiar with the ideal streets to buy on. A fatal mistake out-of-area purchasers make is to only look at the cheaper properties in an area, which can often be on busy roads or in otherwise less desirable sections of the suburb. By living like a local for a weekend, you will get a feel for the area as a whole and the amenities that are important to you.

7. Think about your current and future lifestyle

If you're planning to start a family or you already have young children, how is the property you are looking at going to help you live your best life and enjoy calling it home? Can you build, extend or renovate, or does this property have limitations?

8. Get organised

You can find the property of your dreams at the right price, but you are setting yourself up to fail if you aren't prepared to make a competitive offer or actively engage in negotiations. Don't wait to assemble the right support team; use all the time you have to your advantage. Organise your team so they know you are actively looking and ask them for direction around the best time to engage them when you are getting close to making an offer. They will also guide you as to what to expect and the next step you can anticipate.

9. Know your deal-breakers and deal-makers

As you come closer to making an offer, you will need to make some critical decisions. A common source of issues that comes up is the building and pest inspection report. The inspector who wrote the report will be able to give a detailed explanation about what they perceive to be normal defects for a property of this age or whether there are deal-breakers, such as water damage in the home that can be expensive to remediate. Given your level of inexperience, don't let this cost you the property if you feel scared – find out what the exact issues are and whether they are deal-breakers or bargaining chips that can help you seal the deal.

10. Make an offer with confidence

Real estate agents will feed off your confidence and your energy. If you can exude a certain level of confidence, they will take notice of you. It is the meek and intimidated buyers who can feel like they are being hustled as the agent knows they hold the upper hand. Don't confuse assertiveness with arrogance, though – stay true to yourself and your style of negotiating. The goal here is to achieve a 'win-win-win': a win for the buyer (you), a win for the seller and a win for the real estate agent. Too often in negotiations the goal is 'win-lose', where one party tries to win by out-muscling the others. Remember, you're all trying to get the same outcome, so being flexible on terms such as the length of the settlement or waiving your cooling-off period can go a long way towards achieving that win-win-win situation.

Who is involved when you purchase?

Finding your property sets off a chain of events that is exciting but can often feel overwhelming. Knowing who is in your team and when they come into the picture will help you enjoy the process and, most importantly, make you feel empowered at every stage of the process.

You

The excitement of your offer being accepted may be replaced by nervousness about what happens next (though your peak fear is likely to be, *Will the bank approve my loan?*). Like all emotions, acknowledge your nervousness and share your concern with your mortgage broker, but accept that your fate is in your broker's and lender's hands and you need to go through the motions to get approved. Allow the process to unfold and try to not let your emotions get the better of you, as everyone on your team has the same focus: getting your loan approved and settling on your property.

Your mortgage broker

The mortgage broker's role is to act as an intermediary between you and lenders, and to assist you throughout the process of securing your home loan. I expand on what mortgage brokers do throughout this book.

Solicitor or conveyancer

You're not alone if you don't understand the difference between a solicitor and a conveyancer. A solicitor is a fully fledged lawyer and can provide legal advice about what structure to use when you purchase (such as a trust or company) and the potential tax implications when you purchase a property. Given their experience, solicitors typically handle more complex property transactions. A conveyancer, on the other hand, is a licensed professional specialist in property transactions in a particular state or territory. Their role is to prepare and review the transfer documentation, conduct title and certificate searches, communicate with the vendor's conveyancer on your behalf and help you deal with any issues that could arise throughout the transfer process.

Whether you choose a solicitor or a conveyancer, make sure you engage them early, such as when you are pre-approved. This will ensure you have time to find out more about their experience, processes and costs, and they can explain their turnaround times for reviewing a contract of sale before you make an offer or attend an auction. Too often I see home buyers leave this to the last minute on a Friday afternoon and expect an instant response. Being prepared and organised will put you in the driver's seat when it comes time to negotiate and if you need changes or amendments made to the contract of sale.

Another helpful tip is not to choose the cheapest legal professional. Why would you want the cheapest legal advice you can get? The power of word-of-mouth referrals is golden, and if you don't have a conveyancer or solicitor then ask your mortgage broker to recommend one to you.

Building and pest inspector

If you are purchasing a house, you will absolutely need to engage a building and pest inspector to carry out an assessment. On some occasions the real estate agent will organise a building and pest inspection report and it is available on request; some home buyers are wary or sceptical of this, but it's important to realise that the building and pest inspector is independent. The goal of the inspection is to identify any issues or problems with the property you are purchasing, such as structural or design defects. An inspector's trained eye and tools will help uncover potential issues such as termite damage, cracks or other structural concerns, water leaks, roofing faults or rising damp. They will not normally check the plumbing or drainage, electrical wiring, appliances or paint.

Once the inspector has completed their check, you will be presented with a 'property inspection report', which is a detailed outline of their assessment of the home's condition and possible issues that need to be addressed or remedied before a sale. These reports must be compliant with the Australian standard, which should give you some peace of mind when it comes to the quality of the report you pay for. If there are issues that need to be fixed up, then the price of engaging an inspector is worth every cent, and you may be able to negotiate the purchase price of the property if you need to undertake some of the repairs yourself. The cost of the repairs isn't usually outlined in the report as this is work that may need a builder to quote on it.

Budget around $500 for this report and factor in about three business days to receive it, depending on the inspector's availability and turnaround times. Spend some time discussing the process with your broker and legal professional so you know when you need to engage an inspector and which inspector you should engage. Ideally, you would engage them during your cooling-off period. They are on your side to help you make a confident decision about a quality property and will tell you if an aspect of the property is a deal-breaker or can be addressed given the age of the property. In the event that the report unearths a deal-breaker issue, then you can rescind your offer on the property, though you may lose a small part of your deposit. If you have already 'exchanged' contracts – meaning you're past your cooling-off period or you have purchased at auction – then you cannot rescind your offer on the basis of the property inspection report.

Valuer

The valuer's job is to examine and give their opinion on the value of a property. Their role and the valuation process as a whole is covered in more detail in chapter 8.

Real estate agents

Your real estate agent plays a central role in your purchase. Along with handling the negotiations on your offer, they will hand you and your legal representative a copy of the contract of sale. If you need to negotiate on the deposit you are putting down, the settlement timeframe or any inclusions in the property, these discussions will be had with your legal representative, the real estate agent and the vendor's solicitor. The real estate agent will also be a helpful point of contact to arrange access for the valuer, and will also be available to you when you do your pre-settlement inspection after your loan is approved and on your settlement day to hand over your keys.

Buyer's agent

Most home buyers have a perception that buyer's agents are too expensive and don't assist much with their search, but you may want to be open to considering a buyer's agent. Even if you have the time to inspect properties yourself, it's important to understand that the odds are not in your favour. You will be liaising with real estate agents who are trained and experienced in the art of negotiating, and you will be trying to bid at auction without much experience. The expertise of a buyer's agent is like an insurance policy for you to avoid making a poor property decision. They can help you with off-market or pre-market opportunities, and even if the vendor decides to go to auction, you may get to see the property before it is listed online and so have a head start over your competitors to do your due diligence and run through your numbers with your mortgage broker. Don't understate the importance of exclusive access to walk through the property, too, as Saturday open homes are busy with other buyers. Your buyer's agent will also be able to handle the negotiations, whether directly with the real estate agent or by bidding on your behalf at auction. Through their research on price and value, they will know how much a property should sell for and how best to make an offer. Do your research and chat with a few buyer's agents to see what their levels and costs of engagement are and whether this is an option you want to consider.

Key points

1. Accept that while this process can happen quickly if you're fortunate, it can often take several months, so you need to strap yourself in and be patient. Most importantly, use that time to your advantage and get yourself as organised and prepared as possible. Also, having those conversations early on about what you like and don't like, and about different property types and price points, can help you narrow down your search.

2. Spend time honing your property strategy by outlining your list of requirements, non-negotiables and where you may have flexibility when it comes to the property you want to buy. Go to as many open homes as possible to build your confidence and train yourself in what to look out for in different properties.

3. Arrange your team of professionals and get organised. You don't ever want to miss out on the opportunity to buy the home you want because you weren't prepared. If you fail to prepare, you prepare to fail.

Chapter 11

How do you work out what a property is worth?

Have you noticed how a property's listed price is rarely the price it sells for? Has the real estate agent misquoted the price, or did someone with deeper pockets simply pay over the odds to buy this home? Warren Buffett has a great quote that's relevant to this (it wouldn't be a finance-related book without a Warren Buffett quote, right?), which is, 'Price is what you pay, value is what you get'. In the home-purchasing context, the price may be set by the agent, and you may be willing to pay this price, but someone else may see more value in this property than you and therefore be willing to pay more. In this chapter, I delve into how to work out what a property is worth and how to do your homework when it comes to determining the value a property has to you.

Why price guides are kind of useless

When you see a property listed online with a price guide, the band is usually set to a 10 per cent range – for example, $500,000 to $550,000, or $900,000 to $990,000. The real estate agent has selected this range according to where they feel the property can be marketed and the ideal buyer they are looking for. Exactly how the real estate agent determines this price range is based on the campaign strategy they have discussed with the vendor – for example, they may set the range on the lower end of the spectrum and then aim to attract a lot of interest in the property and a strong turnout at the open home over the weekend. Agents will often optimise their price guide for buyers who search and filter by price ranges when using online property platforms. This is why it's important to not use the price range filter when looking on property websites as it may exclude some properties that may be suitable for you; search by area, not by price.

Price guides are simply that – a guide. It's only when you engage with the real estate agent and ask about what recent comparable properties have been used to determine the price guide that you will get more of an understanding of how this property price has been benchmarked. Not all properties are created equally – you could have two similar properties with the same number of bedrooms and bathrooms, but if one has a north-facing aspect to the rear and is newly renovated, it's hard to compare it to the other property, which has a poorer aspect and is unrenovated. This is why relying on the price guide can not only mislead you but also cause a huge amount of frustration when the property starts out looking like a bargain only for the price guide to be revised upwards throughout the sales campaign, or the property ends up selling for a price way above the initial price guide.

Underquoting, explained

You may have heard about an illegal practice called 'underquoting', which is when a real estate agent advertises a property for a price that is substantially below market value in order to artificially attract more potential buyers. The line between unethical and illegal can be very fine. During the COVID-19 property boom, the price guides were irrelevant as buyers were paying as much as they could to secure a property. This no doubt led to buyer frustration and finger-pointing at agents for being misleading with their price guides, but ultimately it's how much someone is willing to pay that determines the sale price.

New South Wales Fair Trading issued 161 penalty infringement notices for underquoting and related offences between May 2021 and August 2022, with each agent being fined $2200. Between July 2021 and July 2022, Consumer Affairs Victoria investigated 1466 underquoting complaints, which resulted in just 48 infringements and 171 official warnings issued. It's a practice that even with legislation and fines is becoming hard for regulators to manage and police. In terms of emotional energy, it's going to hurt when you turn up to open homes where the price guide meets your budget only for the property to be sold well above this. I doubt this issue will be resolved anytime soon, so your best bet is to accept this, factor it in when you're looking at price guides and then track every sale for the properties you are keeping an eye on to get a feel for how much above the price guide they are actually being sold for.

Why property reports are helpful but limited

When you begin searching for properties, a great tool to use is CoreLogic's Property Report. This detailed report contains key data for each property, such as sales history, when the property was listed and how long it has been on the market, rental history and, if relevant, any development permit application activity. It also includes photos and floor plans, local school catchment details and data on the suburb where the home is located, such as the number of sales, current median value, changes in the median value, median days on the market, median vendor discount, median asking rent and indicative gross rental yield, if available. The key insight in the report is the 'current estimated value', which is created by an algorithm and based on recent comparable sales. Quite often this value is not indicative of current market value or the price guides as the algorithm cannot factor in how hot the property market is and it uses sales from within the last six months, which is a lag indicator.

When you use this resource to help with your property search, be mindful that these reports aren't definitive when it comes to the price estimates, and they can't factor in unique aspects of the property such as strategic renovations, pool installations or the addition of features such as high-end appliances or solar energy.

Using the 'Sold' feature online

By far the most underutilised feature of realestate.com.au and Domain is the 'Sold' feature. You should regularly search this to find out how quickly properties are being sold, and which agents are selling the properties you are interested in buying and that sold within your price range. If these agents are selling the properties that you are keen on, the chances are that they will get more similar listings, so these are the agents you should proactively contact and introduce yourself to.

A great way to track listings is to create a spreadsheet with the following columns:

- Address
- Number of bedrooms, bathrooms, car spaces
- Land size or apartment internal size
- Condition
- Aspect
- Quality of block/apartment layout (give a rating)
- Listed price

- Link to listing
- Listing agent
- Physically viewed property?
- Sale price
- Days to sell

If the property listing doesn't have a price, sort the listings by price and look at the listings above and below it that do have a price guide, and you'll get an indication of how much the agent has entered into the back end of this online listing. Agents are required to put a dollar amount into the price guide for the online property platforms, even if they want the price to say 'Contact agent' on the front end.

This spreadsheet will become your ultimate tool when it comes to tracking sales and can give you the confidence to cite comparable sales when talking to real estate agents. If you can demonstrate that you are a knowledgeable buyer who has been actively following the market, this goes a long way to being seen as a hot and qualified buyer.

Certain listings will have the price withheld or will say to 'contact agent'. You can call the selling agent to find out how much the property ended up selling for. A possible reason agents do this is to get interest from potential buyers and sellers, providing the agent with an opportunity to have a sales conversation. Some agents may not be able to disclose the sale price as the vendor wanted it kept confidential. A cheeky workaround is to access the valuer general's website for your state or territory and run a search by suburb – this will track all the sale prices, even if they are withheld on the property platforms.

Pre-purchase valuations

Another underestimated resource when it comes to trying to determine how much you could or should offer on a property is valuers. I mentioned in chapter 8 that you can get a valuer to provide you with a 'pre-purchase valuation', also known as a 'pre-sale valuation'. This gives you another unfair advantage when it comes to negotiating as you will have a detailed report from an expert valuer that covers everything you need to know about the property before you agree on the final price. The pre-purchase report will take into account the following details about the property:

- exact dimensions, overall size and land usage
- age and general condition
- location and local government information
- distance to local amenities such as shopping centres, public transportation, schools and parks
- any structural issues that are not council approved or are cause for concern
- parking availability and type, such as double garage carport, or street parking
- the prices of recently sold comparable properties from the last six months.

This can provide you with the leverage to negotiate with the agent and have a quality conversation about the valuer's appraisal of the property. The agent will see the property through the lens of market value, whereas a valuer sees the property from the perspective of a lender, and they may not agree with each other, which is quite normal. Just bear in mind that when you purchase, the bank will order their own independent valuation rather than using your pre-purchase valuation.

For a relatively small price to pay, a pre-sale valuation could help give you some peace of mind about how much to offer and may help prevent you from overpaying for your property.

Key points

1. Do as much research as possible about sales history for the area and the type of home you are looking to buy. Your spreadsheet tracking this data is going to be your source of truth for what properties are actually comparable.

2. Discuss your findings with real estate agents, who have their finger on the pulse of sales and auctions. Great agents love to help potential buyers, and if you can demonstrate that you are a hot and qualified buyer, they will work with you.

3. Learn to use the different parts of online property platforms, such as searching without price filters and scouring the 'Sold' section and property reports. Talk to your mortgage broker about a pre-purchase valuation if you need clarity about how much to offer.

Chapter 12

Buying your home via private treaty

When you do your research about how to buy your home, you will find plenty of online guides, courses, ebooks and videos mainly focusing on getting pre-approved and then finding the property you love. Yet, so little of this information actually lifts the lid and goes deep enough into how the purchasing process works and how to effectively make an offer. It is a unique combination of science and art – there is no standard way to make a successful offer as each purchasing experience is different, but there are some commonalities that you can learn from.

In this chapter, I discuss the process of purchasing a property via private treaty. (The next chapter covers the other common way to purchase a property – at auction.) I also cover how your negotiation style will need to adapt and how to go about doing your due diligence on what price you ultimately want to or need to pay to be successful. This is undoubtedly the most critical part of your property-buying ourney.

Private treaty is perhaps the most common way to purchase property. A real estate agent lists a property with a price, a price range or an amount at which 'offers above' will be considered.

The property is listed and open home inspections are conducted until an offer is made, negotiations are completed and the vendors are happy to accept a final sale price.

Before making an offer

When you attend an open home inspection, you will be greeted by the real estate agent and most likely their assistant or a junior agent, who will ask you for your contact information (your full name, mobile number and email address). This is important as it provides the vendor with some feedback about the number of parties that came through over the weekend and how many are repeat inspections or new visitors through their property. The agents will also give you a follow-up phone call after the weekend, say on Monday or Tuesday, to gauge your interest and ask for feedback on the property.

If you are interested in the property, then the agent will suggest that they send over a copy of the contract of sale. This is often a good place to start as it signals to the agent that you are a hot, qualified buyer. The contract of sale is quite a large document, so the agent will ask for the contact details of your conveyancer or solicitor to email this to them; be prepared by having their name and email address accessible.

The real estate agent may also have a copy of the building and pest inspection report available, which is another vital piece of information you want to review. As I discussed in chapter 10, this report will contain information that needs to be interpreted for you, so feel free to call the inspector who completed the report and ask for their insights and feedback on the property. There is a school of thought that if the report was ordered and paid for by the vendor then it may be biased and not contain the full breakdown of potential issues with the property, but the inspector needs to be neutral in their report as they are putting their name and reputation to it, so they should be disclosing everything they observe in the property. If you are in doubt and want to arrange your own independent building and pest inspection report, then ask the real estate agent if access can be provided for your inspector.

If you purchasing an apartment, then your solicitor or conveyancer will order the strata report on your behalf. I covered the importance of strata reports in chapter 9; this stage is critical for determining whether you are going to proceed with making an offer or not. You will start to feel time pressure from the real estate agent to make an offer or perhaps risk losing the property to another offer, but don't be tempted to cut corners on your due diligence. Take the time to go through the contract of sale, building and pest inspection report and strata report in detail with your legal professional to see if there are any red flags you need to be aware of.

Ideally, you will have done your research on recent comparable sales (as discussed in the previous chapter) and come to a range that you are willing to purchase this property for before making an offer. Recent comparable sales is only one part of the equation, though, as it doesn't account for differences such as aspect, school catchment areas, renovations completed or the potential for future renovations, or features such as a pool or a study, so don't rely solely on this. This is part of why negotiating a purchase price can be an 'art'. There are so many factors to consider, not all of which you can plan for; for example, you may be up against a buyer who has family in the area and really wants to be close to them, which is hard to gauge when you go to make an offer.

Before you engage in the negotiation phase, you want to have a deep conversation with the real estate agent and ask them open ended questions such as these:

- **Why is the vendor selling?** Perhaps they have already bought their next property and hence are very motivated to sell. On the flip side, they might need more time to look for their next home. These factors will determine whether a shorter or longer settlement period will be key in your negotiations.

- **How long has the property been on the market?** This question is optional as online platforms such as realestate.com.au, Domain and CoreLogic can answer this for you. Do your research on the property being listed. Has it been listed with another real estate agency previously? Was it listed and not sold before, or has it recently been sold? If so, this could imply that the property has some concerns or has had a poor marketing campaign in the past, or perhaps the vendors are a little unrealistic about market price. If the property has been on the market for some time, it is certainly worth asking why this is the case.

- **How many contracts have been issued?** This will give you an indication of how many potential buyers and interested parties there are.

- **Have you received any offers as yet?** Buyers have a right to feel cynical about agents being truthful about how many offers they have received and how much has actually been offered, but an agent who chooses to be dishonest at this stage is not only doing you and the vendor a disservice, they are knowingly breaking the law. There is legislation that protects you, the vendor and other potential buyers, though there is some grey area here, which means it's best to be aware of the legalities. Real estate agents are legally obliged to present all offers to the vendor before the contract of sale is finalised. This is important as real estate agents have sometimes been known to not pass on offers to their vendors, which frustrates buyers, but this could be because the vendor has instructed their agent not to submit offers below a certain dollar figure. You have a right to ask the agent for the written offers they have received, but this strategy could work against you as the agent might be less likely to engage you as a serious buyer. Agents may also just say, 'We have a number of interested buyers'. You can ask for a price range of where these offers sit, and a helpful agent will oblige if you ask politely.

Making an offer

Real estate agents spend a lot of time on their phones, so a verbal conversation can get forgotten, and if you make your offer over the phone they may forget the exact offer or who you are. (Don't be offended!) You are required to submit your offer in writing. Here is my suggestion for how to do this.

Hi *[real estate agent name]*,

I'm/We're submitting an offer on [property address]. I/We are already pre-approved and my/our finances are ready to go. Please see below my/our offer to present to your vendor:

- Purchase price = $855,500
- Deposit payable = 5% (this can be transferred within 24 hours)
- Settlement period = Six (6) weeks

Conditions:

- Subject to review of building and pest inspection report and contract of sale
- Cooling-off period = Five (5) days
- Remainder 5% deposit payable after unconditional approval

My/Our conveyancer's details are *[conveyancer's details]*.

My/Our mortgage broker's details are *[mortgage broker's details]*.

I/We can be contacted on [phone number] to discuss this further. I/We want to emphasise that I'm/we're open to negotiations on this and am/are aiming for a favourable outcome for the vendor, for you and for me/us.

Thanks,

[Your name/s]

Bear in mind that this is a template to be used to help you with the daunting step of making a competitive offer. Making an offer via private treaty is a skill that takes years of practice, yet you're expected to perfect it right away. This is why I always recommend engaging a buyer's agent to help you with your home-buying journey. It will cost you money to do so, but if they can help you secure the home you want at the right price and help you stop renting, then it's a relatively small price to pay to guarantee you success.

Once your offer is accepted, this will set off a chain of events that you need to be prepared for:

- **You will need to sign a contract of sale.** Make sure the agent includes your full name (including middle name) and it's spelled correctly. You may read this and have a little laugh, but a misspelled name happens far too often. You may have the option to digitally sign your copy of the contract of sale, or you may need to sign it in person.
- **You will need to pay your holding deposit.** If you are doing this via bank transfer, make sure your daily limit allows you to make this transfer; otherwise, you will need to contact your bank and request an increase to your daily limit. You will transfer your deposit into the real estate agent's trust account.
- **Your mortgage broker will progress your pre-approval to be formally (or unconditionally) approved by your lender.** You may need to provide updated documents such as payslips,

recent bank statements showing your updated savings balance, a copy of your signed contract of sale and the deposit receipt. As I've mentioned, there are quite a few moving parts at this stage, and your first instinct may be to feel overwhelmed. This is normal. Remember to breathe, write down what you need to do and lean on your trusted support team to communicate with one another, show initiative to provide you with updates and let you know timeframes.

- **The lender will order a valuation.** The valuer will contact the real estate agent directly to organise an inspection. You won't be required to attend this. The valuer will then prepare their report, which will be sent to the bank and, usually, to your broker, who can pass on a copy to you. This is the most critical part of your cooling-off period – your loan approval hinges on your valuation coming back in at your purchase price.

This all needs to happen within a five-day cooling-off period, if you're lucky enough to have even negotiated a cooling-off period. Most of the private treaty purchases I see are done by waiving your cooling-off period, which means you need to be even more organised and get your loan approved in advance so you can settle on time.

All states and territories with a cooling-off period have it end at 5 p.m. on the final business day of the prescribed timeframe. Table 12.1 (overleaf) shows each state and territory's cooling-off terms.

Once your loan application has been formally approved, you will then exchange contracts, sign your loan documents and prepare for settlement. This part of your purchase is handled by your legal professional, who liaises with the seller's solicitors. A copy of the exchanged contract of sale will need to be sent to your broker, who in turn will share a copy with the lender to get to settlement.

Table 12.1: cooling-off terms by state and territory

State/ Territory	Cooling-off period	Forfeiture fees*
ACT	Five business days from when both seller and buyer sign the contract of sale.	0.25%
NSW	Five business days from the day when both seller and buyer sign the contract of sale.	0.25%
NT	Four business days from the exchange of contracts.	N/A
Qld	Five business days from when both seller and buyer sign the contract of sale.	0.25%
SA	Two business days from when both seller and buyer sign the contract of sale or when the buyer receives the vendor's statement.	Any deposit over $100 must be refunded in full, while any holding deposits will go to the seller.
Tas.	No mandatory cooling-off period.	N/A
Vic.	Three business days from when the buyer signs the contract of sale.	0.2%
WA	No mandatory cooling-off period.	N/A

*These are fees the seller may impose if the contract is terminated during this period.

Gazumping, explained

Being too slow to make your offer or not making a solid counter-offer can often lead to another buyer 'gazumping' your offer. In this scenario, another buyer offers more and, ultimately, you lose the home and get frustrated at the agent. It's extremely common – most buyers are cynical about whether the real estate agent actually has legitimate offers on the table and think that by holding out, their offer will be successful. This may work sometimes, but do you really want to bet your home on a 'maybe' strategy? You can avoid gazumping by being very clear about your offer and the terms and conditions you are suggesting, but most importantly by being open to negotiation. This doesn't have to mean paying more; it really means you want to work with the agent and the vendor to get an outcome that pleases everyone. Negotiations can happen quickly, so be prepared to give this process the attention and focus it deserves.

The most effective way to avoid being gazumped is to make an irresistible offer, such as by offering a competitive price and waiving your cooling-off period. However, if there is another very interested party, then you can ask the agent, 'If someone else makes a higher offer, will you come back to me so I can have an opportunity to counteroffer?' The agent isn't obliged to, but they will often act in good faith, and if this leads to a higher price then they will definitely come to the party. If you're thinking that the agent is holding out for an extra $10,000 offer, then just remember that in this circumstance their commission will only increase by $200 to $500 on average, which really isn't a lot in the grand scheme of things.

A great question to ask the agent is, 'How much do I need to offer to take this property off the market today?' This signals a strong intent, timeliness and your ability to close this sale efficiently. Before you make your offer, it's worth contacting your mortgage broker and doing your numbers to work out your maximum purchase price.

I always keep coming back to the importance of being prepared, and this level of organisation is critical for your success.

When it comes to making an offer, each property will require a different approach, but never make your first offer your maximum – you need to build in some wiggle room for negotiations. Don't make a lowball offer as these rarely work; rather, look at the price guide and recent sales evidence to pull together an offer you can put in writing to the real estate agent.

What about purchasing off-market and pre-market properties?

There are a number of properties that don't end up on the online property platforms such as Domain and realestate.com.au because they are sold off-market or pre-market. These listings have usually been offered exclusively to a pool of buyer's agents. You can't buy what you can't see, which strengthens the value proposition of engaging a buyer's agent all the more. You may be thinking, *Why doesn't the seller list their property and try to get more money for their property by generating more competition?* There are a few reasons why someone may choose to not have their property listed and run a traditional sales campaign:

- They are private and don't want to let their neighbours, friends or community know that they are selling their property.
- They are going through a divorce and need this property sold, and again, they want to sell their property discreetly.
- They don't want to spend time or money on sprucing up the property by doing any painting, landscaping, small renovations or even property styling to have the home staged for photos, and then clean up their home every weekend for inspections.

- They have bought their next home already and need this property sold as soon as possible.
- They have plenty of time to wait for their real estate agent to find the right buyer and the right price without a formal sales campaign.

With pre-market listings, the vendor is willing to go through with a formal sales campaign and the real estate agent may have completed photographs, but the listing has yet to be uploaded online to the property platforms. Real estate agents have VIP databases where they can invite selected 'hot' buyers to an exclusive inspection of a property before an open home is advertised. This will enable these buyers, who may have previously missed out on purchasing similar properties in this price range, to have a sneak peek and be able to do their due diligence before the rest of the general public. These are brilliant opportunities; you get to enjoy inspecting the property privately and having time to ask the real estate agent as many questions as you like. You may be given a small window in which to make your offer before the agent lists the property online and organises open homes. A great question to ask real estate agents when you begin looking for properties is whether they have a VIP database for hot and qualified buyers. Some agents also have private Facebook groups for these listings, too, so feel free to ask to be added to them.

Settlement

As your settlement date approaches, there are a few things that need to be arranged behind the scenes.

Preparing for settlement

The first step is to arrange for the remaining funds to be transferred to your 'shortfall' account, which is a bank account with the lender your loan is approved with. Your mortgage broker and solicitor or conveyancer will provide you with a breakdown of your 'funds to complete', which is the total amount of your purchase price minus the deposit you have already paid and the loan amount, as well as additional costs such as stamp duty, legal fees, government fees and any extra bank fees. There is also a provision made for utility bills the vendor has prepaid for the quarter and will be prorated for you, including council rates, water, electricity, gas or strata fees. It's important to note that you need to have the funds in the shortfall account with the lender who approved your loan because they will not accept the funds through another institution. Alternatively, you could transfer the funds into your legal professional's trust account, but this should be actioned at least 48 hours before your settlement date.

As your settlement date fast approaches, you also have to do a final pre-settlement inspection of the property you are buying. This is to ensure that it is in the same condition as when the contracts were exchanged. You're ideally checking to ensure that no damage or wear and tear has occurred since your pre-settlement inspection. The exact timing of your inspection will be determined by the availability of the vendor, your real estate agent and what your state or territory legislation stipulates, though it's usually during the week before you settle on your purchase. Some buyers think this is an opportunity to have maintenance issues addressed, but unless it's stipulated in the contract of sale that these issues need to be remediated, you won't have any recourse for repairs to be made. Here is a helpful checklist of things to look out for:

- **Plumbing.** Check the taps are in working order. Also, run the hot water to ensure the heating is operating as it should.
- **Flooring.** Ensure there are no new scratches, stains or other damage you weren't already aware of. You need to confirm if there is a condition in the contract of sale for floors to be steam cleaned as this may not be a requirement.

- **Windows.** Check all the glass windows to ensure none are cracked or broken.
- **Lighting.** Turn on and off light switches to confirm the electrical system is working.
- **Appliances.** Appliances such as dishwashers, cooktops and ovens are all part of the sale, and a quick check of these should confirm they are operational.
- **Blinds and curtains.** Ensure they aren't broken and are not dirtier than they were in your original inspection.
- **Air conditioning systems.** If your home comes with an air conditioner or heater, turn the system on and off.
- **Doors.** Check door locks to make sure they are operational by opening and closing the doors.
- **Pools.** If you're lucky enough to have a pool or spa in your new home, you need to check if the pool heaters or the spa is in working order.
- **Smoke alarms.** You may not be able to test them, but each alarm should have a light to indicate it is operational.
- **A clean condition.** Your inspection should include cupboards, the garage, sheds, wardrobes and under the house to ensure all rubbish is removed, all belongings are taken and nothing is left behind. This may be hard if the vendor is packing and hasn't vacated yet.

For some purchases, you may negotiate some 'special conditions', which could include purchasing the outdoor furniture set or the BBQ, or perhaps removing a shed. You just need to ensure these conditions have been included in your pre-settlement inspection.

Remember, the pre-settlement inspection isn't about nitpicking; you have purchased the property, and this final inspection is to make sure the condition of the property is the same and not worse than your initial inspection. If any issues or questions arise, you need to contact your solicitor or conveyancer.

Settlement day!

This is the day you've been waiting for – getting the keys for your new home! Settlement usually takes place in the afternoon to help you mentally prepare for the day. Behind the scenes, your solicitor, the vendor's solicitor and the lenders involved are working together through an online platform called Property Exchange Australia (PEXA). You won't need to attend the settlement as most settlements happen digitally, the exception being a 'paper' settlement, which is the traditional method of settlement and is quite a rarity nowadays. Your funds to complete will be transferred out of your shortfall account, and you should see your home loan account appear. Once your solicitor has confirmed that your settlement has been completed, your real estate agent will also be notified, and you will then be able to pick up the keys to your home. Understand that the agent cannot hand over the house keys without authority that settlement has been effected, even if you are standing outside your new home with the removalist truck in the driveway.

Most settlements take place on a Friday afternoon, which I personally think is the worst time of the week to settle. I highly recommend having your settlement take place on a Wednesday or Thursday when possible. This gives you breathing space so that if your settlement is delayed for whatever reason, you have a few business days to reschedule. It also gives you a greater choice of removalists and, if required, gives you time to hand over your old place.

Post-settlement

Your mortgage broker will provide you with a loan repayment summary, which will outline your first repayment date, an estimate of this repayment amount and the current interest rate (if it has changed between your approval and settlement). Your broker will also check to ensure the bank has linked your offset account to your home loan account, though I strongly recommend every borrower checks this themselves as well. There have been instances of major banks incurring multi-million-dollar fines for not correctly linking offset accounts to home loan accounts, and it really comes down to personal responsibility. Go into your internet banking and find your loan account, and there should be a tab called 'Account Information', which outlines your current interest rate, linked offset account/s, your repayment date and which account your repayments are coming out of. Put a note in your calendar two days before your first repayment so you can ensure the account that will be direct-debited has a sufficient balance – you don't want to start off on the wrong foot by missing your first repayment. If you are unsure about anything or have questions, please contact your mortgage broker; however, some lenders have strict privacy guidelines that dictate certain account information will not be shared with your broker, in which case you may need to contact the bank yourself.

Your mortgage broker may also undertake a proactive loan review in which your interest rate is reviewed and a request made to reduce your rate if you have had a clean repayment history. This is known as 'repricing'. Some lenders will allow brokers to do this every six months while other lenders allow this every 12 months. (See chapter 14 for a list of various lenders' rate review timelines.) There is no guarantee that they will reduce your interest rate, but it's always worth asking the question.

Key points

1. Familiarise yourself with the private treaty sales process and what needs to happen, by when and by whom in your support team. If you don't have a support team of trusted professionals in place, organising this needs to be your first priority.

2. Learn the art of making an offer (that is, how to engage and negotiate with the real estate agent) and then practice. The more times you try, the more confident you will become.

3. By being open and engaging with the real estate agent, you may get access to pre-market listings, though it is usually only buyer's agents who get access to off-market opportunities. Do some research on buyer's agents in the area you are looking to purchase in and contact them to find out how they can assist you and what their fee engagement and support packages look like.

Chapter 13

Buying your home at auction

With more and more homes being sold under the hammer, it's crucial you understand the auction process – not just what happens at the auction but everything leading up to an auction and what happens afterwards. In this chapter, I go through how to prepare for an upcoming auction, what research you need to do and what happens when you are successful (after you have a celebratory glass of bubbles!).

Auction campaigns are run by a real estate agent to gauge interest in a property in order to get the highest possible price for their vendor. The auction environment is built to emotionally supercharge the bidding process, and it's equally nerve-racking for the prospective buyers and the vendor as there is a lot on the line during the auction process. In contrast to the private treaty buying process, where you may lack some transparency about the current best offer, how many interested parties there are and what price the sellers are willing to accept (known as the 'reserve'), the auction day is the exact opposite: you get to see your rival buyers, who they are, how many there are, how much they want to offer and bid for this home and what the price is to buy this home.

Before we delve into the auction experience, it's worth acknowledging that there is sometimes an opportunity to purchase a property prior to the auction day. Here are some of the reasons why a property might be sold prior to the auction day:

1. The vendors have already bought their next home and need a specific dollar figure from the sale of their home. An auction could be too risky if they don't achieve this exact figure and if a buyer has expressed interest in making a pre-auction offer, then the vendors may not want to risk getting less at auction. They are also now facing time pressure to have their current loan application approved, and a requirement of their formal approval is to show the proceeds that will come from the sale of their home.

2. The sales campaign has not met expectations and buyer interest is poor or waning. With these types of campaigns, it would be embarrassing for the vendor and the agent to go to auction and receive low bids or, even worse, no bids. Then, the balance of negotiating power swings in favour of the buyers. Instead, the agent may push a buyer for an offer and then sell under auction conditions. This means the buyer signs a '66W', which means they waive their cooling-off period, buy unconditionally (that is, not subject to finance or building and pest inspection reports) and exchange contracts immediately.

3. The agent is inexperienced with an auction process. Most real estate agents that run auctions are seasoned experts, but everyone has to start somewhere, right? You may come across an agent who is still quite new to the industry and learning as they go along, perhaps being mentored by an experienced agent. This can play in your favour – seize the opportunity to make an offer and request that they take this to their vendor prior to the auction. You can cite other properties currently

listed that also suit your requirements and that you may be keen to make an offer on.

4. Market conditions, such as the RBA increasing interest rates, could dent buyer confidence or cause some potential buyers to drop off, and the agent or the vendor may not want to risk an auction. They want to close this sale as quickly as possible.

5. The property was never actually going to auction. The agent created a false deadline to drive as much interest as possible, get price feedback and then shop the offers around. This creates urgency, which is critical to a sales campaign. If you ask an agent, 'Will the vendors consider an offer prior to the auction day?' and then the agent either hesitates or suggests you submit an offer, that could very well open the door to pre-auction offers.

Prior to the auction

Preparation and research are crucial for your confidence heading into an auction. This is when you have the contract of sale reviewed, and any changes you need to make have to be requested and approved by the vendor's solicitor prior to the auction day. Some examples of changes you might request include paying a 5 per cent deposit rather than a 10 per cent deposit or extending the settlement period from six weeks to ten weeks. You also need to review the building and pest inspection report in detail and identify any potential issues, as once you bid and successfully buy, there is no opportunity to withdraw from the purchase. You absolutely need to have your pre-approval (also known as 'conditional approval') organised and ensure you have run and re-run your numbers with your mortgage broker to work out the absolute maximum you can afford to bid for this property. You can also discuss whether your parents will be contributing any additional money towards your purchase to ensure this is factored in. Another point to chat about with your mortgage broker is your lender's current turnaround times: some lenders will experience delays at certain times in the number of days it takes them to assess and approve loan applications, and knowing this in advance will help you mentally prepare for the time it can take for your loan to be formally approved.

I discuss in more detail in chapter 11 how to research the potential value of a property, but remember that auctions bring out the emotional side in buyers, so what your research may indicate in terms of market value may not necessarily equate to what someone is willing to pay when it comes time to bid. I often say to potential buyers that there are four prices for a property:

1. how much you're willing to pay
2. how much your competitors are willing to pay
3. how much the vendors want for their property
4. how much the real estate agent has promised to sell the property for.

You don't know any of the last three numbers, so all you can control is the price you are able and willing to pay for this property. Before you head into the auction, you want to be very clear about your purchase price range. The three numbers you want to have in your head are how much you want to pay ideally, your comfortable upper limit and your absolute stretch price. The question you want to ask yourself is, *How will I feel when I wake up the morning after the auction if I missed out on buying this property because I wasn't prepared, even though I potentially could have afforded it?* Then, think about how frequently your ideal property comes onto the market, how long you may need to wait until a home like this is listed again and where property prices could be by then.

A great question to ask the real estate agent is when to register for the auction. Simply asking this will elevate your status in the agent's eyes as they will let the vendor know how many registrations there are before the auction day, and you are helping to boost this number. You will need to bring identification with you on the day of the auction and collect your bidding paddle.

Having your deposit organised is also very important in the lead-up to an auction. The first question people frequently ask is, *How much should I organise a bank cheque for?* Usually at auction you are required to pay a 10 per cent deposit, which can either be in the form of a bank cheque or a bank transfer. You will need to go into a bank branch to organise your bank cheque, and you will also need to work out how much the cheque needs to be for. Don't fear if the bank cheque is not exactly 10 per cent of your final purchase price, as it can be over or under; you will then be able to reconcile the difference between your deposit paid and your loan amount when you are getting your loan formally approved. If you opt for the bank transfer, then you need to make sure your daily limit allows for this amount.

Doing your research by attending as many auctions as possible is absolutely essential preparation. You get to see first-hand how the auctioneer likes to create a sense of urgency, engage bidders and then control the bidding process. Each auctioneer will have their own unique style but, ultimately, they want to speed up the auction to encourage more active bidding. Watching auctions on YouTube is a great way to also see how buyers react, their body language and the cues of the successful bidders, such as their ability to confidently bid and also where they choose to stand in relation to the auctioneer (usually at the front of the crowd so the auctioneer has a clear line of sight to them). If you've proactively asked the real estate agent who the auctioneer is, then you can jump on their social media platforms as they usually post their auctions there too, and you can get a feel for their specific style of leading an auction.

I often mention that success leaves clues, and you have so many great resources at your fingertips to see what successful bidders are doing to stack the odds in their favour. They are attending the auction early, introducing themselves to the auctioneer and displaying confident body language. These are all new skills you will need to learn, and by going to as many auctions as possible, your fear will slowly dissipate and you will grow in confidence.

Being prepared also means knowing some of the auction jargon. Here is some of the most important terminology to know:

· **Reserve price.** This is the price that the vendors have instructed the auctioneer and the agent to accept as a minimum for the property to be sold at auction. Agents used to say, 'We're on the market', but this is not as common anymore.
· **Seller's/Vendor bid.** The auctioneer may increase the bidding one time to help move bids along if the property has not met its reserve price yet. The auctioneer is signalling that the property has not yet reached the amount the vendors want for their home.
· **Passed in.** The reserve price has not been achieved and the auction has stopped. The highest bidder now can negotiate with the vendors and agent directly to see if an outcome can be achieved.

At the auction

You can cut the tension in the air with a knife at an auction. Everyone has butterflies in their tummies, palms are sweaty and the property is packed with onlookers keen to see what the result is. When did auctions become a spectator sport? All your planning and preparation will come down to this moment and you need to put your best foot forward.

To give yourself time to prepare, arrive early. The property will be open for one final inspection so you can walk around and, more importantly, get a feel for how many potential bidders there are. I would also recommend you introduce yourself to the auctioneer, smile and acknowledge them. This can go a long way towards building some rapport with the auctioneer – it doesn't guarantee success, but the auctioneer came prepared to drop the hammer and get a successful result, so it's all about the one-percenters that stack the deck in your favour. Why not give yourself every advantage on auction day?

When you register, you might be able to see the list of how many other registered bidders there are, or maybe you can ask the person who is taking down the details. As you scope out your competition, you want to see which category each is sitting in:

- **A first home buyer.** They will have a firm price limit in mind, and you'll be able to see when they drop out of the auction from the defeated look on their face.
- **A family who looks like they are upgrading.** These are emotional buyers who may have been looking for quite some time. Perhaps they have family in the area or have been looking for months and may be willing to pay above everyone else for these reasons.
- **A downsizer.** They have sold or are selling their family home and may be quite cashed up. They will know what they are looking for and how much they can afford to spend to outbid others, which makes them quite strong competitors. Just like the upgraders, they may have children or grandchildren close by, which makes them emotional buyers as well.
- **An investor.** They have worked out their numbers and will have a firm upper limit where the investment doesn't stack up and they opt out of the auction.

There is an element of truth to the fact that the bidder with the deepest pockets will win the auction, but with a strong strategy and adequate preparation you can signal to your rival bidders that you are a serious threat and can outbid them. Some bidders may approach the auction with a view to intimidating other potential buyers, but this is not a recommended strategy. Many tactics I see discussed sound more like psychological warfare than sound strategies!

Once the auctioneer completes their introduction and outlines the details for the auction, they will ask for an opening bid. It comes down to your style whether you want to open the bidding or not. If an opening bid is too low, the auctioneer will reject it and politely ask for a more realistic bid. Once bidding is underway, it's a matter of seeing how much the incremental bids are increasing by and the speed at which bids are being made. It is all part of the auctioneer's role to keep bids coming in and moving the price up. If you are going to bid, make sure you raise your paddle and clearly state your bid. With all the people, and sometimes traffic noise, it can be hard to hear, so use a clear, loud voice to communicate your bid. Another tip is to demonstrate confidence by looking the auctioneer in the eye, even if you are nervous. Once you're into the flow, you may find that the first bid was the hardest and your nerves settle after that. As the auction keeps going, some stall, while others may just blow your planned purchase price out of the water. If the auction goes well above your price limit, make peace with the fact that you never stood a chance as someone else wanted it more and was always going to be willing to pay over and above. If you're still in contention, there are a few different bidding methods you can consider, such as bidding odd numbers rather than round numbers or making a bold and assertive bid that is well above the current increment. Some bidders prefer to wait until the very end to make their 'sniper' bid. Your bidding style needs to reflect your style of negotiation and, most importantly, be determined by your budget and how much the bids are increasing by.

If you are successful at the auction, congratulations! You will then be whisked away by the real estate agent to sign your contract of sale and arrange your deposit payment. They may have a chilled bottle of champagne set aside, and after the nerves have settled, a cheeky celebratory glass of bubbles may be in order!

Auction results, explained

On Monday morning you will see the flurry of auction results across various platforms, and the numbers can be helpful, though they may not tell the whole story about the weekend's auction results.

Clearance rates are considered the barometer of buyer confidence and market sentiment, and reflect how a particular area is performing in relation to supply and demand. A good auction clearance rate sits at about 70 per cent, whereas a poor clearance rate may hit as low as 40 per cent. The auction clearance rate equation is as follows:

Properties sold ÷ Total reported auctions = Clearance rate

The figures for properties sold and total reported auctions include each possible outcome: sold under the hammer, sold prior to the auction, sold after, passed in or withdrawn.

It's vital to note that some auction results are not reported for a few reasons. Some agents don't want to disclose that the auction passed in, and some agents have simply not responded to the data collector's request. These situations where there has been no update on the auction result are known as 'uncollectables'. When you look at the auction clearance rates on a Monday, these are known as 'preliminary results' because they are the first set of results to come through from the weekend. By mid-week, with more results coming in, you will find the auction clearance rate has most likely decreased as the uncollectable results have been updated. This is why it's important to look at a few different data sources for the weekend's auction results rather than just the Sunday night news report. A few helpful resources to check out include CoreLogic, realestate.com.au, SQM Research and Pricefinder.

Using a buyer's agent to help you bid

Parents often put their hands up (pun intended!) to bid, but – and I say this with due respect – do they have the experience and expertise to bid on your behalf? They very well could have purchased a few properties through auction, and if that's the case then they would be a perfect candidate. However, if you don't have someone in your corner and you really want to buy this property that is going to auction, then a buyer's agent can bid on your behalf. They will work out your pricing strategy with you in the lead-up to your auction and then work out your auction strategy. The fee you pay a buyer's agent is a relatively small price to pay to help stack the odds in your favour. Just think about a scenario in which you are heading to auction and another bidder comes along with their buyer's agent who knows the real estate agent and the auctioneer – it's a very strong signal to other bidders that they're serious and creates an uneven playing field. Too many times I have seen prospective buyers try to do it themselves and keep missing out on properties, and then they get buyer fatigue and bid over the odds in order to make the home-buying pain go away.

Key points

1. Auctions are a transparent way to purchase property. They require you to be extremely organised and prepared with your finances and purchase price strategy, and engage your legal professional and the real estate agent. Consider engaging a buyer's agent to give you some guidance about what this property may sell for at auction and whether they can perhaps negotiate pre-auction or bid on your behalf.

2. In the lead-up to the auction, have a clear indication of your numbers, including your ideal price range and your absolute maximum purchase price. Do as much research as possible on auctions by attending a number of auctions and watching some on YouTube.

3. Visualise your successful winning bid at auction – how will you bid, what increments will you bid by, how will it feel to see the hammer drop and hear your name be called as the successful buyer, and how will the champagne taste? Seeing yourself as successful is a very powerful tool to help you believe that you can win at auction.

PART III

ENJOYING YOUR LIFE

Chapter 14

Getting on with your life

In this chapter I share a few of my personal philosophies and pointers regarding enjoying life in your new home. Let's pause for a moment and just recognise that living in Australia is truly a blessing – our weather is brilliant, our produce is world class, and our overall social welfare, healthcare and education systems are excellent. No doubt there are some parts of our country that need improving, but when you really put our lifestyle into perspective, it's not a surprise that Australia consistently ranks as one of the best countries in the world to live in. In fact, the United Nations Human Development Index tracks many measures of quality of life and standard of living and ranks Australia fifth globally (as reported by World Population Review).

I cite this to reframe the notion that the Australian property market is inaccessible to home buyers. I agree that it's unaffordable depending on where and what you are buying, but arguing about the injustices of the housing market won't get you anywhere, and the ability to change it isn't in your control. So, what can you control? You can do everything possible to get into the property market and defy the naysayers in the media, who keep peddling articles about how the Great Australian Dream is now the 'Great Australian Scream'. There is a cost, albeit a high cost, to live in one of the best countries in the world, but there are some government grants on offer and other favourable policies that can enable you to make your dreams a reality.

Once you have bought your home

I wish someone had told me about this aspect of buying your own home: how great the feeling is that it's yours. Remember when you bought your first car with your hard-earned money and proudly put your P plates on show? It didn't matter how fancy or not your car was; it was a symbol of freedom and independence. It meant no more relying on parents or friends for a ride, or on public transport. Yes, it now meant budgeting in costs such as petrol, maintenance, insurance and car washes. You suddenly felt that this is what 'adulting' must be like! That's the feeling you get with home ownership.

All the talk in this book about offset accounts, contracts of sale, auctions and loan approvals is important stuff to know. However, what's talked about less, but I feel is more important, is how great that feeling is of being able to say that it's your home. No more having to pay rent and be dictated to on lease terms or rent increases. No more having to ask for permission to put up artwork or have something fixed. No more worrying about your bond being garnished. It's your own home, and you now own a small piece of real estate in Australia. Wow!

The feeling also means friends and family can come over and feel more comfortable knowing they won't risk anything happening to your bond or breach a term in your rental agreement. It means you're able to have a pet without having to ask for permission from a property manager. If you have children, you can enrol them in a school and know that your family has the security of never needing to worry about having to move homes. The roller-coaster of emotions you experience during the home-buying journey – when you miss out on a home you wanted to buy, spend Saturdays driving around to open homes, have conversations back and forth with your mortgage broker and the bank, and negotiate with the real estate agent – they will all fade away and become memories when you get that opportunity to put up the 'Sold' sticker on the signboard. That's the feeling I'm talking about. Think about the excitement of settlement day – holding the keys to your own home in your hands – can you just think about how proud you will be? It's a feeling I want more Australians to experience.

Beware: upgrade your home, upgrade your lifestyle

It's called 'lifestyle creep' – when your income increases, your living expenses and non-essential or luxury spending increase. Think about your first job and how little you were earning then compared to now. You seemed to scrape by, and you managed to juggle your expenses and still find some cash for a night out or a small holiday. Then, as your income increased, the dinners out became more expensive, the cars fancier and the holidays more lavish. The reason it's called 'lifestyle creep' is because it happens so incrementally you don't really notice it, sometimes until it's too late and you're relying on credit cards for purchases.

I have experienced this first-hand. It may surprise you that I'm the spender in my relationship. Bernadette is extremely frugal, whereas I used to place an emphasis on material possessions. It was hard to admit it but when we were saving for our home, I knew our lifestyle had to change, and in particular my spending habits. Being accountable for where your money is spent may sound like being a killjoy if you're the spender. I mean, you work hard, so why not enjoy the fruits of your labour? That's the attitude that inevitably leads to this lifestyle inflation. The discussion Bernadette and I had really centred on what brought us happiness and what we enjoyed doing. We are foodies, so going out for a meal was a treat we looked forward to. So, rather than simply going out, we saved for our dinners out and we only booked when we knew we had the money to enjoy it. The goal wasn't to restrict ourselves but to become mindful of where our money was going. We knew we had a goal to buy our home, and every dollar we saved would go into our home deposit account.

Another great way to reflect on lifestyle creep is to 'act your wage'. It is too easy to live a champagne lifestyle on a beer budget and spend your pay rise before you even get it, to upgrade your wardrobe now that you've got that promotion or new role, or get a car lease because you're told it's more tax effective. However, just because you can do it doesn't mean you have to. A helpful metric for how your budget should be allocated based on your income is the 50/30/20 rule, where 50 per cent of your budget goes towards essential living expenses and your mortgage, 30 per cent goes towards splurge items or wants such as personal beauty products and gym memberships, and the remaining 20 per cent is your savings component, perhaps going towards a holiday or a new car.

Atomic Habits by James Clear is a great book that has so many useful tools and techniques to help you build better habits and become more productive. There is a brilliant story in the book about the 'Diderot effect', which shows that lifestyle creep is not a new phenomenon. Philosopher Denis Diderot came into money and bought a new scarlet robe with his newfound wealth. It was so new and beautiful that it was out of place with all his current possessions, and in his words, there was 'no more coordination, no more unity, no more beauty'. He went on to upgrade all the possessions in his home.

I commonly say that when you upgrade your home, you upgrade your lifestyle. When you purchase something new, such as an outfit, pause before you start buying matching accessories. Being aware is one part of the battle; then, you have to learn to be content with what you have and resist the urge to make unnecessary upgrades.

An antidote to lifestyle creep can be greater accountability to a partner, or maybe a money coach or financial planner. If you don't have access to a planner or coach and you're happily single, then another method is to write down what you want and then come back in a month's time and see if you really still want it. If you've been able to survive a month without it, can you go two or maybe even six months without caving and buying this item? This is a form of delayed gratification; most importantly, it teaches us that buying possessions may not be the pathway to happiness. On the topic of happiness, another technique to avoid lifestyle creep is to be content with what you have already. I love the concept of minimalism, and there is such beauty in the idea that less is more. This may mean buying fewer clothes of better quality, which means you're not having to replace cheaper garments that wear out more quickly. Addressing lifestyle creep also gives you a chance to take stock of everything you have and perhaps sell or donate goods you're not using or don't need anymore, embracing Marie Kondo's KonMari method.

Another suggestion to help you combat lifestyle creep is, when you get a raise, to save the difference of your increase. This way you save all of the additional money and continue to live off your old salary. You can also ask your employer to split your pay into different accounts, which means you won't even see your extra salary come in – it can go directly into your home deposit or savings account. If you have a credit card or buy now pay later (BNPL) debt, then make it a priority to clear this before committing to any new purchases. It's going to take willpower, but your future self will thank you for this. Bonus points if you cut up your credit card and close out the BNPL accounts too.

The RBA has also completed their own analysis of another form of lifestyle creep: the 'wealth effect'. This is when home values increase and the newfound consumer confidence correlates to an increase in new car sales. It is estimated that a one per cent increase in housing wealth is linked to about half a per cent increase in new vehicle sales. Banks know about this too; when I worked at the Commonwealth Bank of Australia in marketing, a statistic I was made aware of was that if someone bought their home, they were 60 per cent more likely to buy a new vehicle within the next six months.

Spend the money on removalists

After all the excitement of buying your home and preparing for settlement comes the onerous task of packing up and moving. This can actually be one of the most stressful parts of the home-buying journey, sorting through what you want to take and using this as an opportunity to do some spring cleaning. After a while, it loses its novelty, and you just end up throwing everything into boxes and declaring that you'll sort it out later. (Then, some of those boxes may just sit unopened in your garage!)

Hands down the best money Bernadette and I spent when we went through our home-buying journey was to hire a removalist company. They packed up our whole house – I'm talking dismantling beds and dining-room tables, folding all the linen, packing up the whole kitchen and moving all the heavy white goods and furniture. They were efficient! All the boxes were labelled and tagged with their contents and which room they belonged in. If you had come to our house two days before we moved, you would have seen that we hadn't packed a single thing. The removalist crew came in the day before, boxed up everything, moved as much as they could into the truck and then, on the morning of the move, finished packing the last items, such as our bed. I recall that when we moved in the past, we were sleeping on a mattress on the floor for a week beforehand because we'd already dismantled our bed! All the fragile items were protected, such as the television, glassware and bottles of wine. What would have taken us two weeks of packing, took this company a few hours with their expertise and efficiency.

I highly recommend allocating a bit of your budget towards a full-service removalist company to pack up and move everything for you. It makes the moving experience so much more enjoyable and less stressful. Think about all the time you will save by not having to buy moving boxes and tape, and then packing and labelling everything yourself. Add a great removalist company to your team of experts and the small investment will be so worth it.

Once you're in your home

The boxes are unpacked, you've found your new local coffee shop and you've even updated your details on the electoral roll! Life in your new home is going great. However, there are a few final things to consider.

Renovating your home

Maybe there are a couple of things that need fixing, or perhaps the way that you like to live isn't reflected in the layout of your new home. Talk of renovating your home comes up – perhaps this was something you identified during the inspection phase when you were planning to buy this property. So, how do you fund your renovations?

There are two key types of renovations: structural and cosmetic. A structural renovation, as the name implies, means changing the layout of your home, perhaps by adding a bedroom or rearranging the kitchen and dining areas. The chances are that the scope of your renovation will be determined by the costs to complete. How much will you be able to borrow from your bank? Do you have the borrowing capacity to undertake these renovations? How much will these repayments be each month? If you've used all your cash reserves to buy your home, then it's likely that your renovations will need to be financed. It's a bit of a chicken-and-egg scenario – do you contact a builder to get an estimate of how much the renovations will cost you and then work out if you can borrow this, or do you speak with your mortgage broker and find out your borrowing capacity first? My suggestion is the latter as you'll need to be guided by your budget rather than getting your hopes up from talking to a builder. Too often I've seen build costs underestimated, which leads to disappointment when you realise you can't complete the work you had in mind. Builders also appreciate an initial ballpark budget to start with and will be pretty clear with you about whether the renovations you have in mind are realistic.

If you are financing your renovations yourself, think of this as you would a construction loan. The builder will provide their plans and cost estimates, which are then passed on to the lender, which will complete an 'on completion valuation'. Bear in mind that there will be some exclusions in the building contract, such as landscaping, fencing and driveways. You will need to factor these costs into your planning with your mortgage broker, as the question will be raised by a lender of how these expenses will be paid. The on completion valuation takes into account your land value, your current home value and the cost to build; once added together, this will give you a value upon completion of your renovations, as the name implies.

A major consideration is whether you need to move out of the property while it's being renovated and rent or live with family. If you do need to rent, then you need to consider this expense. Also, be prepared for timelines not to go to plan. There could be weather events that delay work, building supply issues or delays arising from unforeseen issues in your home. Managing your own expectations is vital to having an enjoyable building experience despite timings and budgets perhaps being stretched. To help with your cash flow, renovation loans typically involve IO repayments, which can just take a little pressure off during this stage; once all your renovations have been completed, you easily can switch to P&I repayments.

Once your valuation has been completed and the bank has approved your construction loan, you will have 'progress payments' to make along the way. Your builder will supply you with an invoice to be paid, you sign this, and then your bank will pay the builder directly. Ensuring these invoices are paid on time is crucial to having a smooth relationship with your builder as they are trying to manage their own cash flow and expenses.

If you're embarking on a cosmetic renovation, you may be managing and overseeing the tradespeople yourself. To finance this kind of renovation, you would likely have been able to access some available equity or secure a small top-up loan, or perhaps a personal loan. The main risk you need to manage during a cosmetic renovation is your budget. If you're halfway through your renovations and you need more money through your lender, they may require a valuation. The lender may be less inclined to approve your request given the property is part-way through a renovation; they don't like giving funding in these situations, even if they hold the current loan against your home.

Don't rush a cosmetic renovation. My suggestion is to go slowly and get as many quotes as possible, starting with the quickest wins you can. The painting, flooring, lighting and possibly gardening are less invasive renovations and mean you may only be out of your home for a small period of time. You could possibly get a short-stay rental such as an Airbnb for a few weeks, allowing you to manage your renovations without overextending yourself financially.

If you are planning on renovating your home, think through how you want to improve your liveability and, most importantly, how your improvements will help with the functionality of your home. To determine this, you may need to spend some more time in your home before rushing into renovations. Here are some other helpful tips to help with your renovations:

- Speak with your real estate agent to find out which home improvements are the most sought after in the area and will add the most value to your home. It may be helpful to look at homes that have sold at a premium in your area and take some inspiration from their improvements.
- Speak with your mortgage broker before you buy that 'fixer-upper' or embark on your renovation plans, as it's crucial you get finances in place at the start of the process rather than requesting more money part-way through your renovations only to be told that your lender won't approve the renovation loan.
- If you need to go through the development application (DA) approval process, give yourself extra time for delays or reworking your plans. It may help to check if you can get complying development certificate (CDC) approval rather than a DA, as this is quicker and easier.
- If you are considering flipping this property (buying, renovating and then selling) in the short term, then you want to focus on the elements of the property that will generate the greatest value uplift. The kitchen, bathroom and garden are where you'll get the best bang for your buck; just ensure you don't overcapitalise on your renovation.

Renovating your home is a great way to improve its functionality and increase its value. By spending the time upfront to work through what type of renovation you are going to embark on and your options for financing, you'll give yourself the best chance of being part of the select few who enjoy going through the renovation process. Allocating a contingency to timeframes and budgets, and thinking through the best- and worst-case scenarios, again provides you with the opportunity to make your project enjoyable and successful.

Comparison is the thief of joy

If you're among those fortunate Australians who have bought their own home, enjoy and celebrate this achievement. Too often we compare ourselves to friends and family who have been able to buy a bigger house or purchase in a superior suburb. When we compare and compete with others, it steals the joy we should have. You have no idea whether those friends were given a substantial cash boost from their parents or received a large inheritance from a family member. You have no idea how much debt they have gotten themselves into. Comparing your home and your life to others' is the start of a slippery slope that leads to discontentment. You've just bought your own home; how many other struggling Australians would give anything to be in your position?

You may try to fill this void by buying more things to keep up or because you feel like you can buy happiness. Happiness is found in gratitude, not in more possessions, and remember, less is more sometimes. If you find yourself becoming jealous, ask yourself why you are allowing yourself to be triggered. Be happy for someone else's success the same way you would like your network to celebrate your milestones.

There are so many useful tools to bring out gratitude, such as journalling, helping others less fortunate than you and shifting your attitude and perspective. I've included this topic because it's a natural human emotion and response to wonder why your peers are sometimes doing better than you, but the chances are that they may actually be looking at your life and wanting something you have. Having the opportunity to call Australia home puts us in such a privileged position in the world, and if you really want to see how truly rich you are, then check out this website, which ranks you against the rest of the world's population based on your income: web.archive.org/web/20200103064843/http:/www.globalrichlist. com.

Reviewing your loan

Your home loan should never be a set-and-forget proposition. Your mortgage broker should have a process in place to actively review your home loan, and you can feel free to ask them about their post-settlement support. Some lenders will allow your loan to be reviewed and your rate renegotiated every six months, while other lenders will review your rate annually. Table 14.1 provides a summary of the lenders that I work with and how frequently they will allow a rate review (information accurate at time of writing, November 2023).

Table 14.1: lenders and their rate review timelines

Lender	Rate review after 6 months?	Rate review after 1 year?
AMP	No	Yes, every 3 months, subject to lender's approval
ANZ	Yes, subject to lender's approval	Yes, subject to lender's approval
Auswide Bank	Not usually, but may do on a case-by-case basis	Yes (on a case-by-case basis)
Bankwest	Yes	Yes
Better Choice Home Loans	Yes (on a case-by-case basis) – no limit on number of requests	Yes (on a case-by-case basis) – no limit on number of requests
Better Mortgage Management (BMM)	No	Yes

Lender	Rate review after 6 months?	Rate review after 1 year?
Bluestone Home Loans	No	Yes
Bank of Queensland (BOQ)	Yes, they are happy to consider genuine retention reviews as they arise	Yes, they are happy to consider genuine retention reviews as they arise
Commonwealth Bank of Australia	Yes	Yes
Connective Essentials (Advantedge)	No	Yes
Connective Select (Adelaide Bank)	Yes, subject to lender's approval	Yes, subject to lender's approval
Connective Solutions (Pepper Money)	Yes	Yes
Connective Resolve (Thinktank)	Yes, subject to lender's approval	Yes
Connective Elevate (Bluestone)	No	Yes
Firstmac	Yes	Yes
Gateway Bank	Yes, they can allow as early as 3 months, subject to lender's approval	Yes
Heartland Bank	No	No
Heritage Bank	Yes, subject to lender's approval	Yes, subject to lender's approval

Lender	Rate review after 6 months?	Rate review after 1 year?
ING	Yes, subject to lender's approval	Yes, subject to lender's approval
La Trobe Financial	Yes, subject to lender's approval	Yes, subject to lender's approval
MA Money (formerly MKM Capital)	Yes, subject to lender's approval	Yes, subject to lender's approval
Macquarie Bank	No	Yes
ME Bank	Yes, subject to lender's approval	Yes, subject to lender's approval
National Australia Bank	Yes, subject to lender's approval	Yes, subject to lender's approval
Pepper Money	Yes, subject to lender's approval	Yes, subject to lender's approval
Resimac	Yes, subject to lender's approval	Yes, subject to lender's approval
St.George Bank	Yes, subject to lender's approval	Yes, subject to lender's approval
Suncorp Bank	Yes, subject to lender's approval	Yes, subject to lender's approval
Teachers Mutual Bank	Yes	Yes
UBank (formerly 86 400)	Yes	Yes
Unibank	Yes	Yes
Westpac	Yes, subject to lender's approval	Yes, subject to lender's approval

Your life will certainly change over the next two to three years. The value of your home increasing, your loan coming down a little and perhaps your income increasing will open up opportunities to review and, when required, refinance your loan to secure a lower interest rate. There is a process mortgage brokers follow to ask a lender for a lower interest rate: we provide them with rates being offered by other lenders to see if they will match or beat these rates in order to keep your interest rate as low as possible. If the lender says no or that they are already doing the best they can do, you have the option to call your lender, ask to speak to their retention team and say something like, 'I've just spoken to a mortgage broker and they have offered me an interest rate of 5.25 per cent, but my interest rate is 6.05 per cent. What is the best you can do to lower my rate, or do I need to refinance?' If they don't have the ability to reduce your rate, you can contact their discharge team and, this being their last line of defence to retain your business, see if they have any discretion to lower your rate. A few minutes on the phone could save you thousands of dollars.

If you're on a fixed rate, then it's best to be in touch with your mortgage broker two to three months before your term is scheduled to end. This will give you time to discuss your options, such as whether you stay with your current lender and roll onto a variable-rate loan, fix a portion of your loan or consider switching lender to get a better rate. Your mortgage broker definitely has the responsibility to proactively manage your loan, but if your life is changing or your requirements change from your original engagement, then you can be proactive and contact your broker to have your loan reviewed to make it as suitable as possible for your lifestyle.

Key points

1. The journey to buy your home will be a roller-coaster of emotions and your cortisol levels will increase as you go through a totally new chapter in your life. Be conscious of where your money is going and avoid pitfalls such as lifestyle creep. Live within your means, not beyond them.

2. Don't rush to renovate as soon as you move into a new property. Live in your home for some time and see how you live there, the spaces that you use, what you like and don't like, and what can and can't be changed. Also, be realistic about how much budget you have for a renovation and the impact any renovations may have on the value of your home.

3. Being a homeowner is an achievement you should be proud of and celebrate. Don't lose that joy by comparing and competing with others; run your own race. The only comparison you should be making is comparing your loan to what other lenders are offering to ensure your interest rate is as competitive as possible.

Acknowledgements

Having a young family, you realise why 'it takes a village to raise a child'. To all our family members – Mum, Dinuke, Shaun, Larry, Rani, Damien and Lily – thank you for all your help being part of our family's journey. I sincerely thank you for all your support of the business since I launched Atelier Wealth seven years ago, with me being away to write this book, and believing in what we're doing.

To the wonderful team at Major Street, thank you so much for your encouragement and support. I'll never forget the day when I mustered the courage to call Lesley Williams out of the blue. I didn't expect you to answer, and when I pitched you my idea for this book, your response was 'Great, can you send over two chapters?' This ignited the flame in me to put pen to paper and take the thousands of conversations I'd had with hopeful home buyers to craft a book that would deliver on its promise. Thank you to Will Allen and Eleanor Reader for your wonderful support and creative flair, too – you have been instrumental in bringing my concept to life.

There have been so many people who have contributed to my journey, and I'm extremely grateful for the role you have played in my life. To Glen Carlson and the Dent Community for championing the power of the entrepreneur, you do amazing work. Glen, that breakfast at Bondi literally changed my life – thank you, mate. To David Dugan, Nick Farrow and the incredible Abundance Global community, thanks for celebrating our success and helping us think bigger than we could have envisioned for ourselves. To my best mate, Angus, who hosted me in Chiang Mai while I spent time writing this book – we had such an incredible time together, and I appreciate not only our friendship but the bond we share.

To all our clients at Atelier Wealth, thank you for entrusting us to be your mortgage broker of choice. With over 18,000 mortgage brokers across Australia, I still pinch myself when we have clients refer their friends and family to us. You took it upon yourselves to personally recommend us, and we want to repay your loyalty by showing up to be the best versions of ourselves. Thanks for your ongoing support of our business, and I can't wait to see your lives unfold and watch you all prosper through property.

To our team at Atelier Wealth, you are such an incredible bunch of humans, and you truly make this culture what it is. The way you all show up and contribute sets such a high standard, which I know we are proud of, and we don't compromise on this bar we set for ourselves. Thanks for your trust in us and for staying the course of our mission to help more Australians buy their homes, grow their property portfolios and build intergenerational wealth through investing in property. We're just getting started.

Last but not least, thanks to my wife Bernadette and our two girls, Sienna and Zara. To be blessed with you all in my life makes me rich beyond measure. Bernadette, you encouraged me when I may have doubted myself, and you were there to get me refocused to power ahead. What we have been able to do together over the last ten years of marriage makes me proud and excited about what the future has in store for our family. To my daughters, Sienna and Zara, you have come into our lives and made us so happy and grateful to build a life together. Thanks for all your encouragement and support to make the dream of this book come true.

Glossary

Assessment rate: A higher interest rate than the actual interest rate of your loan, which lenders use to 'stress test' your serviceability.

Assets: Possessions, which may be expected to increase in value (such as property or shares) or lose value (such as cars).

Body corporate: The governing body of a block of apartments or town-houses. They manage the common areas.

Capital growth: The appreciation in value of an asset over time.

Cash flow: Money coming in (income) or out (expenses). Positive cash flow is when more money is coming in than going out, and negative cash flow is when more money is going out than coming in.

Cooling-off period: The period after signing the contract of sale when you can withdraw from the property without facing legal repercussions.

Conveyancer: A specialist in the transfer of property ownership between parties.

Credit score: A rating of your perceived ability to fulfil financial commitments.

Debt: Borrowed money, which generally accrues interest at a rate set by the lender.

DTI: Debt-to-income ratio, a measure of your monthly debt payments divided by your gross monthly income. For example, a DTI of 1:6 on an income of $100,000 per year means you can get a loan of $600,000.

Equity: The value of your ownership of a property. For example, if you have a property valued at $600,000 and a mortgage of $400,000, then you have $200,000 or 40 per cent equity in that property.

Interest rate: The price paid for borrowing money, expressed as a percentage over a period of time (for example, 5 per cent per annum over 30 years). A fixed interest rate never changes, whereas a variable interest rate may move higher or lower over time.

IO: Interest only, a type of loan whereby your repayments cover only the interest on the loan and you do not pay down any of the principal.

Lenders: Entities that lend money that you must then pay back, usually with interest. They include banks as well as nonbank entities.

Liabilities: Things that you owe to other parties, such as personal loans.

Lifestyle creep: An increase in spending in line with an increase in income.

LMI: Lenders mortgage insurance, which protects the insurer from financial loss if you are unable to meet your home loan repayments. Commonly, you are required to pay LMI if your LVR is lower than 80 per cent.

LVR: Loan-to-value ratio, showing the size of a loan relative to the value of the asset the loan is being used to buy. It is expressed as a percentage; for example, an LVR of 80 per cent means that the loan is 80 per cent of the value of the asset.

MPI: Mortgage protection insurance, which protects you from financial loss if you are unable to meet your home loan repayments.

NOA: Notice of assessment, a statement that explains how your tax assessment is calculated.

NSR: Net surplus ratio, comparing your income with your expenses to determine the surplus amount available for you to pay your total debt commitments.

Offset account: A transaction bank account linked to your home loan. The money in this account is used to 'offset' your loan balance; for example, if you have a home loan balance of $500,000 and $20,000 in your offset account, interest on the loan is calculated on $480,000 (the full loan balance minus the contents of the offset account).

Overcapitalisation: When the cost of renovating a property exceeds the increase in the property's value from the renovations.

P&I: Principal and interest, a type of loan whereby your repayments cover both the interest (the fee you pay to the bank for giving you the loan) and the principal (the original amount borrowed), so the size of your debt is reduced over time.

Pre-approval: When a lender agrees in principle to lend you a certain amount of money towards the purchase of a property.

Principal: The total amount borrowed from a lender.

Rentvesting: An investing strategy whereby you live in a property that you are renting while renting out a property that you own.

Serviceability: A lender's assessment of your ability to meet repayments on a loan.

Strata fees: Fees paid to the governing body of a block of apartments or townhouses to contribute to the maintenance of the common property.

UMI: Uncommitted monthly income, your net income after expenses (including loan repayments).

References

Preface: A home loan is a privilege

Honda, K, *Happy Money: The Zen path to a happier and more prosperous life*, Penguin Life, 2019.

Clason, GS, *The Richest Man in Babylon*, Hawthorne Books, New York, 1955.

Chapter 1: How to mentally prepare yourself to buy your dream home

The Australian Financial Review, 'Rich list', accessed 7 December 2023, afr.com/rich-list.

Gardner, S & Albee, D, 'Study focuses on strategies for achieving goals, resolutions', press release, Dominican University of California, 1 February 2015, scholar.dominican.edu/cgi/viewcontent.cgi?article=1265&context=news-releases.

Parkinson, CN, 'Parkinson's law', *The Economist*, 19 November 1955, economist.com/news/1955/11/19/parkinsons-law.

Ferriss, T, 'Why you should define your fears instead of your goals', video, TED2017, April 2017, ted.com/talks/tim_ferriss_why_you_should_define_your_fears_instead_of_your_goals.

Orr, S, 'Compromising lifestyle to purchase property is buyers' biggest regret', Compare the Market, 22 February 2022, comparethemarket.com.au/news/compromising-lifestyle-to-purchase-property-is-buyers-biggest-regret/.

Chapter 2: How to save for your deposit

Australian Bureau of Statistics (ABS), 'First home buyer loans fell to five-year low in January', 3 March 2023, abs.gov.au/media-centre/media-releases/first-home-buyer-loans-fell-five-year-low-january.

CoreLogic, 'Home Value Index up 0.8% in September as demand/ supply imbalance continues to push values higher', 2 October 2023, corelogic.com.au/news-research/news/2023/home-value-index-up-0.8-in-september-as-demandsupply-imbalance-continues-to-push-values-higher.

Galloway, A & Malo, J, 'More than 70% of young people believe they'll never be able to buy a home', *The Sydney Morning Herald*, 26 February 2023, smh.com.au/politics/federal/more-than-70-percent-of-young-people-believe-they-ll-never-be-able-to-buy-a-home-20230223-p5cn01.html.

Hamilton, D, 'Does your brain distinguish real from imaginary?', 30 October 2014, drdavidhamilton.com/does-your-brain-distinguish-real-from-imaginary/.

Chapter 3: Understanding your borrowing capacity

Atelier Wealth, 'Mortgage Repayment Calculator', accessed 7 December 2023, atelierwealth.com.au/calculators/repayment/.

Chapter 5: Lenders mortgage insurance – friend or foe?

Burke, K, 'How much have property prices risen over the past 30 years?', *The Sydney Morning Herald*, 31 August 2022, smh.com.au/property/news/how-much-have-property-prices-risen-over-the-past-30-years-20220830-p5bdwa.html.

ABS, 'Average Weekly Earnings, Australia', May 2023, abs.gov.au/statistics/labour/earnings-and-working-conditions/average-weekly-earnings-australia.

Iliakis, N & DuBose, E, 'What is the average rent in Australia in 2023?', Mozo, updated 5 December 2023, https://mozo.com.au/home-loans/articles/what-is-the-average-rent-in-australia

CoreLogic, 'The long game … 30 years of housing values', 29 August 2022, corelogic.com.au/news-research/news/2022/the-long-game-30-years-of-housing-values.

Chapter 6: Guarantor loans, explained

'Being in the business of the "bank of mum and dad"', *Life Matters*, radio program, Australian Broadcasting Corporation, 1 November 2023, abc.net.au/listen/programs/lifematters/the-bank-of-mum-and-dad/103047738.

Wootton, H, 'How much money are parents lending kids to buy houses now? Take a look', *The Australian Financial Review*, 29 November 2023, afr.com/companies/financial-services/the-bank-of-mum-and-dad-is-good-for-70-000-new-analysis-concludes-20231129-p5enpp.

Hughes, D, 'Bank of Mum and Dad in trouble as young borrowers struggle', *The Australian Financial Review*, 14 October 2022, afr.com/wealth/personal-finance/bank-of-mum-and-dad-in-trouble-as-young-borrowers-struggle-20221011-p5bovh.

Binsted, S, 'Bank of Mum and Dad statistics 2023', *Finder*, updated 16 June 2023, finder.com.au/bank-of-mum-and-dad.

Hazra, A, '"Bank of mum and dad" the biggest factor in young Australians entering property market, research finds', *The Guardian*, 21 March 2023, theguardian.com/australia-news/2023/mar/21/bank-of-mum-and-dad-house-support-young-australians-property-market.

Chapter 8: What happens during your loan application?

Lonergan Research, *Property Possibilities: Buyers' Outlook Report*, May 2021, aussie.com.au/content/dam/aussie/documents/news/aussie-property-buyers-report-may-2021.pdf.

Chapter 9: Property types

Mulcahy, S, 'Buyers spend average of nine months searching for new home', realestate.com.au, 22 March 2019, realestate.com.au/news/buyers-spend-average-of-nine-months-searching-for-new-home/.

St.George, 'St.George kick-starts Australian dream for first home buyers', media release, 13 July 2020, stgeorge.com.au/about/media/news/2020/13-july.

McGrath, J, 'What key amenities are worth', McGrath, 17 July 2023, mcgrath.com.au/advice/articles/john-mcgrath-what-key-amenities-are-worth.

Chapter 10: The home-buying experience

Allianz, 'Buying a home impacts the mental health of one in two Aussie buyers', 16 October 2019, allianz.com.au/about-us/media-hub/buying-a-home-impacts-the-mental-health-of-one-in-two-aussie-buyers.html.

Lontayao, R, 'Homebuyers reveal what causes stress when purchasing a house', Mortgage Introducer, 21 March 2022, mpamag.com/uk/mortgage-types/residential/homebuyers-reveal-what-causes-stress-when-purchasing-a-house/399297.

Mulcahy, S, op. cit.

Chapter 11: How do you work out what a property is worth?

Cassidy, C, 'Underquoting in Australian real estate industry is leaving buyers feeling betrayed', 27 *The Guardian*, August 2022, theguardian.com/business/2022/aug/27/underquoting-in-australian-real-estate-industry-is-leaving-buyers-feeling-betrayed.

Chapter 14: Getting on with your life

World Population Review, 'Standard of Living by Country | Quality of Life by Country 2023', accessed 7 December 2023, worldpopulationreview.com/country-rankings/standard-of-living-by-country.

Clear, J, *Atomic Habits: Tiny changes, remarkable results: an easy and proven way to build good habits and break bad ones*, Avery, New York, 2018.

Gillitzer, C & Wang, JC, 'Housing Wealth Effects: Evidence from New Vehicle Registrations', *Bulletin*, Reserve Bank of Australia, 17 September 2015, pp. 13–20, rba.gov.au/publications/bulletin/2015/sep/2.html.

Global Rich List, accessed 19 December 2023, web.archive.org/web/20200103064843/http:/www.globalrichlist.com.

About the author

Aaron Christie-David is one of Australia's leading mortgage brokers, ranking in the prestigious Mortgage Professional Australia (MPA) Top 100 for four consecutive years between 2019 and 2022. He and his wife Bernadette co-founded one of Australia's premier mortgage broking companies, Atelier Wealth Mortgage Brokers, which has been recognised with numerous industry awards, including Brokerage of the Year at the Australian Mortgage Awards and Best Boutique Independent Office in NSW at the Better Business Awards.

Aaron's career spans marketing and financial services, and he uses this experience to bring Atelier Wealth Mortgage Brokers to life. In addition, Aaron has also launched the *Australian Property Investment Podcast* for property investors looking to build intergenerational wealth through property investing. He has been featured in *7NEWS* and *9News*, *The Australian Financial Review*, *Bloomberg*, Domain and realestate. com.au, sharing his insights on the property market and the mortgage industry.

Aaron has an undergraduate degree from the University of New South Wales (UNSW) and a postgraduate degree from the Australian School of Business. He is a member of the Mortgage and Finance Association of Australia (MFAA) and is involved in industry initiatives such as the Opportunities for Women initiative, and mentors new mortgage brokers to provide them with a pathway into the industry and ensure they have successful careers.

Index